From Misery Alley to Missouri Valley

From Misery Alley to Missouri Valley

My Life
Stories
and
More

Reza Varjavand

To order additional copies of this book, contact:
Xlibris Corporation
1-888-795-4274
www.Xlibris.com
Orders@Xlibris.com
61471

Contents

Acknowledgment

Without the unprivileged kids of my childhood community, Maydan Mir, I would not have had the inspiration to write my life stories. I think of their lives as candles that burn continuously to brighten the lives of others. I would like to express my gratitude to them and wish them all well wherever their lives have taken them.

I give special thanks and heartfelt appreciation to my beloved parents. They both passed away a long time ago. But may they rest assured that no matter what the impact this book may have in leading others to deeper understanding, it is dedicated to their everlasting love and memory.

I am grateful for America, a country that has allowed an immigrant like me to take a dream birthed in poverty and bring it to actuality.

Most of all I want to acknowledge my love and gratitude to my wife Maryam for her unfailing support. She put up with me all these years in loving marriage, and especially during the time when I was writing different pieces of this book. I also lovingly thank my delightful kids, Melody, Nader, and Nathan. Without their patience and sacrifice this project would not have been possible. Their lives have enhanced mine immensely.

I thank Sister Rose Wiorek, RSM for her editorial service.

I also thank those who read online the preliminary version of many of the pieces of this book and made helpful comments.

Introduction

"The act of writing is an act of optimism. You would not take the trouble to do it if you felt it didn't matter."—Edward Albee

When I was visiting my native country of Iran a couple of years ago, I was fortunate to have been given an invitation to do a presentation at a local high school in my hometown. It was indeed a cherished and somewhat adventurous opportunity for me because I had not done any presentations to high school students before, let alone in Farsi, my native language. When I entered the big room where the presentation was to be given, I met a large group of enthusiastic students between the ages of 16 and 18. Because high schools in Iran are gender-segregated, the students were all boys. I had prepared nothing for them in advance because the invitation was spontaneous; consequently, I decided I would be spontaneous, engage them in conversation, and see what would develop. I began with some introductory remarks and then I thought I would capture their attention by asking them a question. I told them that good teachers are good story-tellers; they tell all sorts of stories in order to stimulate their students' engagement in the subject matter and to get important points across. Then I asked the question, "Do you know what the most important story is that you can tell?" A few of the students raised their hands. One of them happened to be in the front row; his hand was higher than others,' and I could tell from his facial expression that he had an interesting answer for me so I let him speak. He said the most important story a person could tell is *the story of his life.* His answer was not only remarkable but also unexpected because it was given by a 16 year old boy. I tried to imagine how many noteworthy life stories this very young man could tell; in any case, his answer set the tone for the rest of my presentation. I began to speak to the students about my own high school experience here in Iran when I was their age.

From that time on, I have often thought about this young man and his answer. This experience eventually led to my decision to gather together some of the things I had written in my spare time over the course of a few years and publish them in the form of a book. The content of this book is comprised of memories and some reflections on my life experiences from when I was growing up in Iran, as well as, musings on some contemporary issues of the day from my perspective as an economist, or a Muslim, or as an immigrant parent raising children in the United States.

I believe the words of Edward Albee quoted above. The act of writing is an act of optimism and I do it because I believe it does matter. For me, the optimism Albee refers to is similar to President Barack Obama writing about his audacity to hope, and this book is the result of my daring to dream. When I look back on my poor younger years in Iran as one of seven children of illiterate parents, my journey at times seems almost unimaginable. It was my great good fortune to have been the youngest of four sons born to my farmer father; therefore, I was not needed to help with the farm so I was freed from that filial responsibility. This freedom allowed me to dare to dream. My curiosity and love of learning drove me to work hard and to strive for something more—coming to the United States, becoming an economics professor at a Chicago university, and raising bicultural children.

The second part of Albee's quote is just as meaningful; I took the trouble to write because writing does matter. I believe that communicating one's experiences, thoughts, and opinions with others is one side of an essential conversation that has been going on since the dawn of civilization. Cavemen began this communication and conversation when they first felt compelled to share the pictures of their lives, and their world at that time, on the stone walls of their homes and gathering places. This conversation has continued through the ages and is one of the lynchpins and benchmarks of human civilization and culture. The medium of writing invites the reader to see through the eyes of another the simple accounts of ordinary things, and in so doing hopefully deepen their awareness of diversity, stimulate thought, and ignite imagination. This book, even though it is my own personal sometimes lighthearted version of life and contemporary issues rather than a scholarly tome, is an expression of my desire to contribute my voice to this age-old conversation.

I am grateful to you for taking the time to read this book. I hope you find it interesting, humorous at times, perhaps thought-provoking, and well worth your precious time. Even though one's childhood memories are his or hers alone, sharing them with others can be an immensely rewarding experience for the writer and the reader. Recording one's memories can help foster an appreciation of one's life as well as inform others about who we are and how we got to where we are now. Reading the thoughts and opinions of others can also help bring to light important issues that may otherwise remain unnoticed, provide a different perspective on things, and invite disagreement and/or further discourse. I leave you with a popular image put forward by Max Gropius, an authoritative guide on research and writing: "The human mind is like an umbrella. It functions best when open." I invite and welcome your openness to what lies within these pages.

Part I

From Misery Alley to Missouri Valley

Our No-name Alley

A lthough it has been a long time since I was in high school, I still remember this always-applicable sentence from my Arabic textbook: "Knowledge earned at a young age is like carving in stone," it lasts for a lifetime. Indeed, what we learn during the early stages of life will be with us forever, and will shape and nurture our personality and beliefs throughout our entire existence.

I spent my childhood years in a small, poor neighborhood in the city of Qum, Iran called *Maydan Mir (Mir square)*. It was during these crucial years that my life's story began to materialize and the most memorable period of my life started and ended. I never could forget that place. Sometimes, especially at night when I can't sleep, my mind, like the swiftly soaring falcon, flies far away back to that place, roaming the sky above the roofs of the houses of that community. When I think about it now, I realize that Maydan Mir was not the place for everyone. Only a small group of people, those who were at the bottom of the social caste system, lived in this community. They were connected not by a social club, a central air conditioning system, or a computer network, but through daily prayer at the mosque, religious holiday ceremonies, and the mourning of the dead. Most of these people were farmers, construction workers, bus or carriage drivers, restaurant owners, tradesmen, or bazaar merchants. One could easily notice how their strenuous daily work had taken a crippling toll on most of these people because they were prematurely handicapped. Rough facial skin, premature white hair, and intensely darkened skin due to extreme sun exposure, were all common signs of debilitating daily work.

Even though my father was a farmer, there was no sign of any trees or other plant life in our house, nor was there any trace of life enhancing amenities. Frankly, our yard was not big enough for anything to grow. There was only a homegrown fig tree that had no benefit for us; its only purpose seemed to be the collection of dust on its leaves which caused rashes on our skin, coughing, and itching. Our disoriented life in this house resembled the fate of passengers in an automobile going down a hill with no brake system. The inability to control our destiny forced us to accept the idea that our fate was predetermined and we had no choice but to submit to the flow of time.

My parents were completely unconcerned about the bleak future awaiting them. Their existence in this world was believed to be preparation for the next. Indeed, they viewed their temporary life as a prelude to eternal life after death. As a matter of fact, they were looking forward to the end of their mundane earthly life as the joyous start of their eternal life. If your life was comparable to absolute suffering, how could you wish otherwise? They really believed that the world was similar to a prison for pious people. Issues of justice or injustice, comfort or hardship, having or not having, victory or defeat, pride or humility, and upward mobility didn't seem to matter to them or even exist. They had no admiration for anything except their religious beliefs. Their belief was so intense that I sometimes viewed them as hostages to their own faith. They were like the soldiers living in a world in which permanent peace was guaranteed; nothing challenged their life. Their view of life left me with nothing to hope for. One good thing about my parents was that I didn't have to strain my mind to understand them because their lives were so simple and their thoughts so one-dimensional. Whether I agreed with it or not, I always admired their integrity and devotion to what they believed was their purpose in life.

It was not a good time to be growing up as a kid. There were no signs of modernity in our neighborhood; life was simple, primitive, and deprived. Basic necessities such as electricity, running water, and mass communication were considered foreign to us. Where I lived, even asphalt was an unattainable luxury. During the months of winter, when you walked on the muddy surface of the long and narrow alleys, you would sink into sticky mud up to your ankles.

In fact, not a single day would go by without someone slipping and falling on the slippery surface and getting injured. There was no shortage of shortages in our community and the most persistent one was the lack of money.

The nameless alley in which our house was located was elongated and narrow; it was not too kid-friendly because it was not suitable for any kind of fun and play. The people who lived in our alley were all poor farmers except for one family whose house was the very first one to the left when entering the path. The head of that household was a man who was a member of the clergy, a sheikh. For this reason we called him *Agha* (Mr.) *sar chooche-e* as if there was no other agha in our alley. I remember when he would come out of his house, all the women who happened to be sitting and gossiping outside would double check their chadors to make sure that they were covered properly.

There were tall, extensively muddy walls enclosing our alley on both sides. The length of these walls would remind me of my geometry teacher who told us that two parallel lines never intersect no matter how long you extend them. Even though the classic example of this concept was railroad tracks, for me, however, the everyday example was these two hideous walls. When you looked at these walls from the start of our alley, you could hardly see where they ended.

Unluckily, our house was at the very end of this alley. That meant that when it came to filling our *hose*—a concrete in-ground pond—with fresh water, we had to wait until everyone else had their turn. Every community around us had a person who was in change of channeling running water into the neighborhood through streams—most of them muddy, some of them concrete—usually after midnight in order to be sure that all the people and animals were asleep and the possibility of contaminating the water was slim. He was called *Joob pa*, the stream watcher! Because our house was the last in line to get fresh water, my family had to bribe him handsomely anytime we needed to fill up, otherwise, we may not have gotten our fair share of fresh water. My father used to say that filling our hose with water was more difficult than *amal omme davood*, a very long and difficult religious ritual.

The only things that still connect me to that house are my memories; there is nothing else worth holding onto. By today's standards, our house could be compared to a huge backyard shed situated at the end of an undeveloped plot of land. The house was very old and built completely out of clay and mud walls that caved in or caved out. No colorful object was present in this house. Khaki was the color scheme of our interior decoration. The house had only two bedrooms. One room was the place in which we actually lived, *otagh neshiman*, or the living room; the other room, which was built on top of the big in-ground pond, *hose*, was extremely humid and practically uninhabitable. Thank God, we decided to use the other room to live in and sleep in, otherwise, who knows what would have happened to our health because of long term exposure to moisture and humidity. Our bathroom, which was called *zaroori* (necessary) by my father, was built at the far corner of the yard so as to keep the bad smell away from us. Using this bathroom was really a sport, an art, and washing your bottom afterwards was a tedious religious responsibility. We had to take turns using the bathroom in the morning. This is how I learned my Macarena dance! At the entrance of our house was a lengthy strip of roofed dark space called *dalloon,* or covered alley. The attic space at the top of dalloon was the place where we stored wheat and barley. The adjacent space was reserved for the storage of animal food for our cows and donkeys. We called it *kahdoon.*

Under our only living/bedroom was a basement that was more frightening than Abu Ghraib prison. It was dark and so dusty that even roaches didn't want to make it their home. The only things you could find in this basement were very old farming tools, many of them obsolete even by the standards of those days. In a corner of our front yard was a small room, which was our kitchen. We called it *matbakh* which means place for cooking in Arabic. The inside of it was so gloomy and depressing it made me think of the devil who is supposedly in charge of the daily punishment of the worst sinners in hell! The soup and meat stew pots, *dizi abghossht,* were always boiling in our kitchen. I remember that when I returned from school in the evenings, I was really hungry and kept bugging my mother for food. Because it was too early for the family dinner, she would take a big piece of bread and dip it into the boiling *dizi* and give it to me. The absorbed floating fat made it so memorably delicious. As part of her daily routine, my mother had to boil a huge pot, *ghazghoon*, of milk every day to make yogurt. Selling yogurt to the only local grocery shop in our neighborhood was one of the key sources of income for our household. She had to carry the heavy pot of milk up many stairs to the kitchen. She had to seek help from *jaddeh sadat,* the prophet Muhammad, many times over.

The only entrance to our house had its own unique personality. It was covered with heavy hardware and the door was so onerous that only a man of great strength could fully close it. There was no lock or any other safety system to protect the belongings in our house. As a matter of fact, we didn't need such a system. Finding anything worth stealing in our house was as scarce as finding a picture of a pious Mullah next to a beautiful woman in bikini! The "computerized" locking system of our house was called *caloon doneh*. The only thing you needed to open the entry door, if it was locked, was an L-shaped piece of wood. This piece of wood was like a generic key that could most likely have opened every door in our alley. Every now and then, someone was bitten by a snake or stung by a scorpion as he/she tried to reach deeply into caloon doneh to open the door. For this reason, it was one of the things I was really afraid of doing. Some of the scorpions in our house were more frightening than *ghashieh* snakes that live only in hell.

There were no postal addresses on the houses in our alley primarily because the alley itself had no name. The person who delivered the mail in our neighborhood was a friendly gentleman named Mirza Abbas Ali, the only micro-grocer in our quarter. Almost all of the postal letters and packages were addressed to him, so he had the pleasure of reading the letters before delivering them to the intended addressees. He was aware of the content of almost all the letters sent to us because he was one of the few people in the town who could read. Most residents, especially the older ones, could not read or write. It was Mirza Abbas Ali's social and moral duty not only to deliver, but to read the letters to the final recipient. I was always thrilled when we had a letter because I loved to save the stamps.

One of our next-door neighbors, Mashdi Asghr, was another typical poor farmer living in our neighborhood. His continuous, loud and irritating coughing did not motivate him to give up his habit of smoking his tobacco pipe, *chopogh*. After His first wife died a few years back, Mashdi Asghar decided to marry again, *tajdid farash* (repeat marriage, so to speak). This time he married a younger woman, as we used to say: *saroon piri, maareke giri*. His first marriage resulted in the birth of a few children. His eldest daughter Zahra, was physically smaller than most of the other girls her age. This was the reason she was nicknamed *Zara moushe,* which literally means she was as big as a mouse! Giving nicknames to people, although often despised, was not unusual in our town; it helped to differentiate kids. As a matter of fact, kids as well as adults were more recognized by their nicknames than by anything else. Zahra use to come to our house to learn Quran from my mother who was kind of like a home teacher as well as a sitter for kids. Even though my mother was formally illiterate, she was fairly skilled in reading Quran just like many other individuals in our neighborhood and in our country for that matter. She had a few other girls like Zahra enrolled in her Quran exclusive class. Zahra was a smart student. I remember that she had finished *amme joase*, a brief section of Quran prepared for freshmen, in just a few weeks. Her accomplishment gave her parents immense joy. To express their appreciation, Zahra's parents brought a big jug of goat milk for us, 100% pasteurized! Because teaching Quran to others was a moral duty for every believer like my mother, the children in our neighborhood, especially females, were able to receive a tuition-free education. My mother had no expectations of pecuniary reward. However, the parents of the students often sent my mother alternative tuition payments such as: wheat or barley, yogurt, dried fruits, *mohr and tasbih and other* souvenirs they brought back with them from holy places like Karbala. Regrettably, I heard that Zahra was later killed in a traffic accident. God bless her soul.

I was fascinated watching these innocent female angels who were sitting down in a row at the front of *rahl*, a decorative book holder made out of wood, and moving the upper part of their bodies in sync while reciting the verses of Quran together. While they had no understanding of the meaning of what they were reading, they were mesmerized by the sheer power of the words and the rhythm of the short verses they were chanting together in harmony.

The Rhythm of Life

If Afghanistan is the poorest country in the world and Nigeria the most religious, my Iranian community was like Afghanistan inhabited by white Nigerians! With the exception of a few, our neighbors were not monetarily any better off than we were. Most of the other houses in our neighborhood were not fancier than ours. Privacy was not safeguarded in our community; personal and confidential information would be disclosed routinely. We would know almost everything about our immediate neighbors, from garlic to onion, so to speak.

The house next door to us served as the home for two families. Mashdi Esmaeel was in his sixties and lived in one half of the house with his wife and many kids; his sister Fatemeh Sultan and her kids lived in the other half. After their father died, the brother and sister decided to divide the inherited house by building a wall through the middle of it, thereby creating two sections. This solution was much easier than going through time consuming government bureaucracy and costly legal hassles. But it was like South and North Korea geographically and attitudinally; the brother and sister and their families never got along in a civilized way. I always wondered how so many kids managed to live in such a small house. The number of kids in that house, as a matter of fact, was larger than the number of times the Pope has apologized for the sex-abuse scandals created by the bad behavior of Catholic priests!

Fatemeh Sultan was our most memorable neighbor. She was an outspoken old lady who lived with her only adult son and her daughters. She was nicknamed *aroos sara khatoon*, the bride of madam Sarah. I never saw her husband Mr. ooch ghorboon, perhaps because he died before I was born, or maybe he ran away because he could no longer stand Fatemeh Sultan's monotonous talk and bossy attitude. She was an interesting old lady though. Sometimes when she saw me outside, she would call to me and offer me a few pieces of candy or a hand-full of roasted watermelon seeds which she would take carefully out of a corner of her huge head scarf. You see, the head scarf was not solely for covering one's hair and respecting Islamic dress codes. It was also a convenient holding place for cookies, candies, and house keys. Often when her son was not home, she would ask me to bring her a jug of fresh cold water from *ab anbar*, a huge in-ground storage tank that was filled with water and somewhat isolated. The winter made the water very cold and it remained very cold for our use throughout the summer. I received much personal gratification from doing such a simple act of kindness which, of course, was not without monetary reward. Fatemeh Sultan was more than happy to offer me one or two Rials (Iran's unit of currency) in return, but I usually refused to take the money because I didn't want to spoil the nice feeling that came from being altruistic. I only wanted to enjoy the praise and gratitude she showered on me for being a Good Samaritan. For me, there was no rationale for using charitable acts as a means to make money!

Abanbar was the source of cold drinking water for the residences in a community. It was a kind of in-ground semi-vertical tunnel with a high arched entrance called *sardar*, and a long stairway that allowed access to the water at the bottom of it. The sardar was the outward manifestation of the importance of abanbar. It was usually decorated with colorful, immaculately designed pieces of ceramic tile at the top and the name of the main donor was inscribed in the middle. It was an admirable sign of distinctiveness for every community. The height of its entrance and the number of stairs it contained were two key criteria for determining an abanbar's importance. Comparing and ranking abanbars of different communities was a fun activity for kids to engage in; it became like a research project for us. Children from different communities would brag about their abanbar and engage in spirited arguments concerning which one was better and bigger. Often adults had to intervene to help resolve such strategic issues which were considered so vital to communal pride and prestige. Our abanbar, as I recall, had close to 30 stairs. A person had to walk down 30 stairs in order to reach the big faucet at the bottom of the stairway that was connected to the water reservoir. Going down with an empty jug was not a tough job, but climbing back up 30 stairs with a filled jug was really labor intensive. Once you reached the top of the stairs, your breathing would be so heavy that you couldn't count the number of breaths you were taking. Unfortunately, abanbar was a safe place for obnoxious kids to do something that they should have done in a toilet! Luckily the odor left by such activity was partially offset by the strong musty smell of humidity that always hung heavy in the air. We use to say that the more crowded the abanbar, the larger the number of jugs that may accidentally be broken! But on a more positive note, a crowded abanbar was probably much cleaner because kids could not use it as their private bathroom!

The kids who lived on our block and played together were deprived and came from poor families like the "children of a lesser God." They were all in the same poor economic situation as me, *aas-o-paass,* as we use to say. I always thought that if we lived next to wealthy people (*aayoon*), feelings of shortcoming, desperation, and disdainfulness would have overwhelmed me. I always wondered about how wealthy people, who could afford to buy bicycles, nice clothes, and fancy toys for their kids, reacted emotionally when they saw our baggy pants (*tomboon*) and our toes sticking out of our worn rubber shoes (*galesh*). What kind of feelings did they experience? Did they feel sympathy, apathy, or maybe even shame?

I thought I was lucky to be living in a town where I could study at night under the public light poles that were installed in the main wider alleys and in the streets. I considered this to be our share of the public service provided by the government only we didn't have to pay for it directly. I could also study under the dim orange light of the kerosene lantern that we used at night as our main source of light; often we would also use it for cooking, simmering, or keeping the food warm. However, using the kerosene lantern for study was not a wise thing to do because I thought the cost was a drain on my family's budget, and the light and resulting heat would irritate others and deprive them of a restful sleep.

Often the viciousness and horror of fate or bad luck would strike our community mercilessly, such as on the day the youngest son of one of our neighbors drowned in their deep covered pond (*hose*). The mourning and crying of his mother was loud and unending. I remember women in black chadors attending the boy's funeral and offering their condolences to his mother ZanHaji. I thought ZanHaji was partially responsible for this tragedy; her son's death could have been prevented if she had been more careful in caring for him. I also remember the night our only milking cow died after weeks of illness. The agony of losing her was unbearable for us. It was like losing a member of the family. For me, a young kid who brushed the cow every day and helped my mother to milk her in the evenings, even the thought of losing her was inconceivable.

In those days, it was normal for boys to follow in the footsteps of their fathers and pursue his profession. Luckily, this norm did not apply to me because I was the youngest child; I was the youngest of seven children to be exact. As such, I had more freedom to choose and do other things like go to school. Even though I had a strong desire to study, the continuation of my education and my advancement from one level to another was never part of a long-range plan; it was simply a year to year decision and totally unpremeditated. My parents allowed me to go to school as long as I did not sacrifice my religious beliefs by submitting to and being taken over by *oloome bi dini* (anti religious science)! I can never have enough appreciation for my older brothers. They worked diligently everyday as mechanics or farmers, but they also facilitated my daily attendance at school and gave me two Rials almost every morning. This gift from my brothers was my lunch as well as my dessert money. It was sheer pleasure for me, and a few other students, to spend our lunch money to buy *aash* (soup) and bread at a place called *bazaar kohneh* (old bazaar). Two Rials was enough to cover my lunch as well as the dessert *ab bargeh or bamieh*!

A huge piece of odd-shaped land named *Maydan Mir*, was the focal point of our community, its business district, and its recreation center. A mosque and a big rectangular building called *takyeh* were located side by side at the south end of this land. This big open area was also the place where children played team sports, especially *marreh bazi* which was kind of a generic version of baseball. We played this game using a hand-made ball similar to modern baseballs. Shops that supplied our everyday necessities were scattered irregularly around the square; some of these included: two small grocery stores, a shoe repair store, *pineh dooz*, a tea house which was our kind of Internet café, a *halvaei* store (the owner was nice enough to offer me a summer internship), and a public bathhouse.

In those days, fancy toys and toy stores were financially out of our reach. We had to make our own toys using our own imaginations. Imagining and creating our own toys gave true meaning to the phrase "toys are us"! The most popular toy, which was also my favorite, was *sim charkh* (wired circle). In order to make it, we first had to find a used tire, and then we would burn it and take out the two metal rings that remained after the tire was completely burned down. Those rings are inserted into the walls of the tire by the manufacturer to strengthen the tire's ability to absorb pressure. After we took out the metal rings, we would make a nice custom handle from thick wire and attached it to the ring; the toy was now complete. We enjoyed many hours of fun rolling the ring by holding on firmly to its handle, and pushing it forward on the surface of streets or the main alleys. The sim charkh would be in front of us and we would be behind it. It was both fun and sport, plus it was an activity that took us to different places within our town. It was especially enjoyable to roll the sim charkh on asphalt roads. The kids used this toy for drag racing which was our favorite pastime.

Tribute to My Parents

While the real story of some people's lives may begin with a scandal or with love affairs, my parents' story began with a marriage devoid of any scandal or adventurous romance. I am sure my father had not seen my mother before their marriage; this was not unusual at that time nor is it unusual even today in many places. Of course, there was no love at first sight. Their marriage was a blind marriage that was arranged and brokered. Traditionally in Iranian society, marriage was considered a social contract rather than an affair based on love. Consequently, the two families involved negotiated the contractual terms and conditions meticulously. It is really hard to imagine what your love life would be like if you married a person you didn't know or hadn't even seen before. Remarkably their marriage, which was typical, lasted for a lifetime; the words "until death do you part" were a lived reality. This gives some credence to my own theory that love is not the guarantor of a marriage and the necessary and sufficient condition for its continuance; the guarantors are mutual patience, devotion, commitment, and unselfishness. My parents must also have believed that gradually love and friendship would follow the marriage and it seemed like these did.

Those days were a really difficult time in which to be a female because women were not allowed to make many choices or have much flexibility with what they did and how they did it. For a woman, being in love with a man or even contemplating such an idea was something that would have stained the family name, and was considered disrespectful to the sacred institutions that Muslim society had honored for centuries. Having a female child was already considered a burden for a poor family, so it was no surprise if parents rejoiced when they sent their daughter to her new husband's home. Often parents experienced a sense of relief because an economic burden had been lifted; a major expense had been eliminated from their budget. For women, it was a religious duty to marry at a young age and to raise good kids, kids with strong religious values that would keep them from straying from the straight path. Such values would be instilled in children at a very young age by their mother.

My mother, like other women in our community, managed her life fairly well and seemed to feel fulfilled. Family matters would be resolved easily and peacefully. Women didn't have, of course, much negotiating power since they were expected to be obedient and subdued; the attitude of submissiveness was required of them by tradition and sanctioned by religion. It was, therefore, an

implicit understanding that women should submit to men and to
the institutions that were believed to be God-given; no one should
dispute the validity of this understanding or try to alter it. I can't
envision what would have been the topics of my parents' discussions
at their dinner table (*sofreh*). The "dinner table" on which their food
was served was a long piece of plastic or cloth spread on the floor.
I have a suspicion that they may never have had any discussions at
all about important social or political issues. Whatever the issues
might have been, politics was not on their minds. Complex matters
including marital issues, if there were any, would be resolved
through mediation facilitated by a respected relative or an elder
(*rish sefid*) whose verdict was final, and the parties in the dispute
would comply with it. Such arrangements seemed to have worked
well, especially for younger couples.

During my childhood, women had their own chat club. They
usually gathered at the front of one of the houses in our alley; they
would sit on the porch and talk for hours (*ekhtelat*) while doing
the daily household tasks and analyzing the day's events. It was
like a generic version of the television program *The View*. Almost
any issue could be put on the table and analyzed except for matters
related to their intimate life with their husbands. Women in those
days were much more reticent when it came to talking about their
private life. Obviously, men were not allowed into this women's
club. The presence of men would hamper the women from talking
unreservedly about issues, especially those strictly pertaining to

women, and make them feel uncomfortable because men were *na mahram*, the term used to refer to a man who is not a close relative of a woman.

Despite economic hardship, my father seemed to be fully content with what he had. I don't remember ever hearing him complain about any deficiencies. He was a devout Muslim in the real sense of the word which means total submission to the will and word of God. After each daily prayer he declared his satisfaction with whatever fate God had determined for him. He was illiterate; nonetheless, he would recite many of Koran's *Soureh* relying solely on his memory. I remember that every night before going to bed, he would recite aloud several verses from the Koran seeking God's forgiveness and guidance. The highlight of his bedtime prayer was to reaffirm the legitimacy and the inevitability of death by repeating this famous verse: "We come from God and to him we return." He steadfastly resisted the temptation to indulge himself in impulsive worldly pleasures in exchange for eternal gratification in the next world. Often, in my simplistic mind, I wanted to ask him to please not talk about death and the punishment of judgment day (*azab e rooz ghiamat*) so persistently. I was worried that I would develop a bleak mentality from prolonged exposure to the talk of death and harsh eternal punishment.

I can remember vividly my father adamantly defending his simple life and his pride in the fact that he attained everything he possessed through his own diligent efforts, *aragh jabin va kde yamin* as he used to say. Conceivably, that was his only defense for what I considered the despondent life we had to endure every day. It was always perplexing to me why so many people in our community lived in unbearable conditions, but did not appear to be unhappy or have any desire to change things.

Although there were typical disagreements between my parents regarding many issues, there was no conflict between them when it came to how they raised their kids, especially the moral code and standards they expected us to follow and respect. They were very meticulous in instilling and reinforcing in their children good moral and ethical values and they held us to high standards. This was one of the key goals of their lives. We kids often disliked their treatment because it seemed harsh and even embarrassing at times, but they believed that being strict and consistent was an integral part of being good parents. Even though they were strict and illiterate, they were considerate and very knowledgeable about life's important matters. My parents did not do for me any of the things that are expected of modern parents today. They never drove me to school, obviously because we didn't have a car. They did not read me books at my bedside simply because they could not read. They did not buy me toys, take me to dinner at a restaurant, or spend any true quality time with me; but they were good parents and that was what mattered. My deep reverence for them never allowed me to challenge their decisions, be irresponsible toward their feelings, or raise my voice when talking to them. I sincerely believe that I had the best parents in the entire world and never felt that I needed better ones.

In those days, it was not customary for the sons of the family to move away. Sons were supposed to stay at home or nearby and be a source of support for their parents when advancing age made them unable to care for themselves. Like other older men, my father was at the mercy of his sons after he got older and could no longer work; his eldest son, my oldest brother, was traditionally obligated to take care of his aging parents.

A hand-written document, a reminiscence of their marriage, is the only nostalgic thing left for me of my parents. This document was prepared by a mullah who, I assume, conducted my parents' religious marriage ceremony (*sigheh aghd*). It dates back to 1339 *hejri ghamari* (lunar calendar); that would be more than ninety years ago according to the lunar calendar. My mother's dowry back then was fifty *tooman* which is equivalent to five cents by today's standards. Eat your heart out Heather McCartney! My parents' marriage certificate which is now on display in my family room was mysteriously found by my cousin; he gave it to me when I visited Iran a few years back.

My parents were lifelong members of the unprivileged class, a class of people which were consistently ignored, pushed to the margin of society, and coerced into an impasse. These people had virtually no voice when it came to social issues; they had no control over what had been decided on their behalf, or where they were heading in life. The sad realization that my parents, like many other poor people in this world, didn't have a voice has generated in me a sense of resentment and frustration. These feelings compel me to stand up and speak out on their behalf. Speaking out on poverty and injustice is a way in which I can pay tribute to my parents as well as honor their experiences, struggles and sacrifices. Standing up and speaking out is a way for me to demonstrate that I am here to represent them and their generation. They didn't have a voice back then because society denied them a voice and continues to deny poor people a voice, but I can stand up now and be their voice and hopefully claim for them the recognition that they were denied but so justly deserved.

The Islamic Ordination

During my childhood, one of the distinct signs of the social worth of a local community was the existence of shops that sold essential food items, especially a butcher shop and a bread bakery. Our community *Maydan Mir* lacked both of these shops, so we had to travel everyday to adjacent communities to buy our daily dietary necessities which included meat and bread. I was the one who was given the responsibility of performing this unpleasant task. I would have preferred to be a dog rather than go to other communities and shop! People in these other communities treated me as if I were a second-class citizen. Sometimes when I would be walking back home carrying the bread I had bought, a large piece of the bread would be ripped away from me by the native kids; taking a portion of my purchase was like a kind of "excise tax" imposed upon me because I was a non-resident. Meat and bread were relatively inexpensive at that time; however, they were allocated through non-price rationing mechanisms such as friendship with the seller. People had to buy their meat and bread early in the morning otherwise they would have to do without them that day. Thank God the butcher knew our family. We had the honor of being his self-proclaimed friends and because of this he was nice to me. He also sold meat to us on credit because my father's credit rating was excellent; he was poor but credit worthy. Our daily allowance was 2.5 *seer* of meat which contained almost 40 percent fat; we used this to make delicious broth. For us, eating steak was a mistake! While I do not remember what the exact weight of one seer was, I think it was a very small fraction of a kilo, perhaps about 7.5 percent of a kilo. Anytime I went to buy meat, I had to carry with me a smooth plank of wood that was about a foot and a half long. This plank of wood was like a prehistoric form of a monthly statement called *choobkhat*. It was a very important item since it was the only document we had that showed the number of times we purchased our daily allowance of meat. Such transactions were almost entirely based on the honor system, so it was not unusual that the butcher trusted us with the safekeeping of the choobkhat. Every time we bought meat, the butcher would make a v-shaped cut on the surface of the choobkhat; this was like debiting our account for the value of the meat. It was also the butcher's way of recording and counting one transaction. Payment for our purchases was due usually at the end of a one or two-month period and was calculated by multiplying the value of each transaction by the number of cuts, or transactions on the choobkhat.

Our community for the most part had friendly relationships with the other communities surrounding us. However, there was one smaller community named *Pnaje Ali* that was at odds with us and it was located near to our house. Nobody envied the families that resided on the border of two adjacent communities that had a hostile relationship. We were like *choob do sar naje* (a piece of twig with two dirty sides); we were neither fully welcomed by Maydan Mir nor by Pnaje ali. The reasons underlying the unfriendly relationship between these two communities were political as well as logistical in nature. First of all, Panje Ali was a community with very little political clout because its population was so small. Secondly, this community could not assist in meeting any of our essential needs, so we had to travel to other neighboring communities to buy bread, meat, fruits, or to go to the public bathhouse. Pabje Ali was not located in a strategically important area either. We didn't even have to walk through it to go to the focal places in the central district of our town such as the grand mosque, repair shops, or other businesses. In summary, we had no vital interests in that community. Additionally, Panje Ali was not big or powerful enough to support us in any potential conflicts we might get into with other adjacent communities. In those days, it was also customary and a kind gesture of support for the people living next to your community to attend your important public events, such as mourning of the religious imams during the month of *Moharram, aza dari,* political rallies, parades, and funerals.

Panje Ali's residents were never willing or able to lend a hand to help us make such events more successful.

Occasionally, a "preemptive strike" or confrontation was initiated by some trouble-seeking kids of Maydan Mir against Panje Ali that often resulted in a group fight. I remember kids from Maydan Mir would march toward the center of the Panje Ali community carrying with them "weapons of mass destruction" like slingshots (*Tirkamoon*) and chanting patriotic slogans such as: "Down with Panje Ali," "Death to Agh Shokrolla" (the political head of Panje Ali), "Maydan Mir's kids are as brave as the male lion," or "Panje Ali's kids are as dumb as a foal, *Korreh Khar.*" The humanitarian purpose of such attacks was to free the people of Panje Ali from an oppressive regime headed by a dictator, and to spread badly needed democracy in that community; but the mutual end result was casualties that included broken skulls, wounds and bruised bodies. At the end of these fights both sides would claim victory as is done in the wars between Palestine and Israel. In reality, the real winner of such fights was usually determined by the number of injuries inflicted and the number of casualties suffered by each side; the number of broken heads was the most decisive factor. The gang fights would eventually end because of the intervention of adults acting as peace brokers, or often they just ended at the chanting stage much like the verbal altercation between the United States and Iran over issues related to nuclear energy.

One of the memorable places at the center of our community was a rectangular building that served as a sort of residential school for young theology students (*Tollab oloom didni*), or students of religious jurisprudence. That building, I remember vividly, was as noisy as the floor of a modern day stock exchange, especially during evening hours. There were heated group discussions among the *Tollab* on religious issues, or heated discussions of the core chapters of their freshman textbook which was entitled *Jaame Al Moghaddamat* (a basic textbook on Arabic grammar), or some senior students were loudly practicing their art of *rozeh khani* (public preaching). All of these loud, passionate activities were preparation for the job of public preaching which the students ultimately sought.

My mother was never stubbornly insistent, but she made it known that she wanted me to become a theology student, or at least to have close relationships with members of the clergy. After a few casual encounters, I was able to establish a friendly relationship with a potential member of the clergy; he was a rather handsome young man who was also *Sayyed*, a descendent of the prophet Muhammad. I will call him Mr. H to protect his privacy. I liked him because he was moderate and reasonable when expressing his views and he embraced modernity. He even kept a radio in his room which was a religiously prohibited item for a theology student. We also knew his family. My friendship with him was actually my sly response to my mother's request that I establish relationships with the theology students. I was in my late teens and in high school at the time; he was perhaps two or three years older than me. I would to go to his room occasionally in the evenings after I returned from school. I use to discuss with him and the other young theology students who came to his room various social and spiritual issues from the perspectives of science and religion. Often we engaged in never-ending debates on issues; the philosophical nature of such issues resulted in an inability to find scientifically valid answers. Occasionally, our discussion was interrupted and eventually ended when my mother showed up with a kerosene lantern in her hand calling to me, "*nane to hanooz injaee*, (Are you still here my dear?)" showing her anxiety and motherly care for me.

When the time came, Mr. H invited me to his *Ammameh Gozaroon* ceremony. It was really interesting to me. It was like a custom-made personal graduation party or a crowning of a prince, *Taj Gozari*. The pre-rolled black turban that was placed on top of his head by a high-ranking ayatollah amidst the jubilation and chanting of *Slavat* (salute to the prophet Muhammad) by the audience, fittingly contrasted with his bright-skinned face. I am sure Mr. H is now a high ranking member of the clerical elite in Iran. I tried to find him the last time I visited Iran but it was to no avail. I wasn't certain about how he would react to my visit. I wasn't even sure how he would receive me after so many years, or my pursuit of a dichotomous career path, or my possible contamination by Western culture.

Like other buildings in our community at that time, the residential theology building had no electricity. Just as we did at home, Mr. H. and other students had to use a kerosene-burning lamp called *Gerd Sooz* for light and for study at night. Perhaps the Farsi proverb *doode cheragh khordan* has its origin in their experience. One night I was deeply inspired by this situation and composed a poem with this starting line: "I envy the night gathering at the dormitory of theology students whose party light is a Gerd Sooz lantern" (*be shab neshinie tollabe din baram hasrat—ke noghle mahfele anha cheraghe gerd sooz ast*). Mr. H., who was also a talented calligrapher, wrote the entire poem very nicely and posted it on the wall. I wish there had been a copy machine back then so I could have photocopied the poem for myself. I am certain that if this handwritten piece was in existence now, it would be a highly-prized national historical document. My friendship with Mr. H. continued even after I entered Tehran University for undergraduate college education.

It was a dream of most of the theology students to eventually become a professional preacher (*Vaaez*). Becoming a popular preacher was not automatic. It mainly required that one be endowed with several personal attributes: the ability to deliver convincing public sermons, a good voice, a bit of a sense of humor, comprehensive knowledge of Islam's holy book Quran as well *Hadith* (the oral narratives supposedly related to the utterances and deeds of the Prophet Muhammad), and a God-given passion

for public speaking. It usually took several years of hard work to
gain enough experience to develop all or most of these skills and
attributes.

Having inadequate experience and an unknown reputation
made it difficult for a novice cleric like Mr. H. to get frequent
invitations for *rozeh khani*, especially in important places or
for important occasions. In an attempt to help him get "a jump
start" on becoming known and getting established, I told him he
could come to our house for rozeh khani which was sponsored
by my mother on monthly basis. He was delighted to accept this
invitation and promised not to let me down. On his first day, he
came on time and our house was full of anxious women waiting
for him. Mr. H. delivered a touching sermon about *panj tan*; it
was a bit long but very well received, by the women. As usual
at the end, he switched to reciting the tragedies of *Karbala*, the
martyrdom of the grandson of the prophet Muhammad. Then he
suddenly started chanting an Arabic poem from the opening page
of *Jameol moggadamat*, the freshman textbook on Arabic grammar
which was totally irrelevant. However, no one recognized this
mishmash because the poem was in Arabic and none of the ladies
present knew any Arabic. Unaware of what was going on, they
kept weeping for the suffering of Imam Hossein, the grandson of
Muhammad, and the others who were disastrously martyred in
Karbala nearly 1400 years ago.

When he finished, I prepared to escort Mr. H. back to his room. It was then that I told him, "I believe you messed up at the end of your sermon." and he replied, "Between you and me, I forgot my line."

Revisiting My Roots

My parents must have been in their late 50's when I was born; this rough calculation is based on the fact that they already had six older children. Regrettably, I lost both of my parents a long time ago when I was in my late 20's. My father died 32 years ago. A few years later, my mother passed away. Because I lived in the United States most of my adult life, I missed the opportunity to personally spend much time with them. Visiting their graves when I am in Iran is the only way I can still show my love for them and my appreciation for the many sacrifices they made for me throughout their lives. I believe that paying tribute to one's parents and to significant others even after their deaths, is a beautiful and deeply meaningful moral and religious tradition that we should all cherish. Trying to be mobile and travel in Iran presented difficulties and challenges. Given the chaotic traffic conditions, just attempting to cross streets let alone attempting to drive, are dangerous things to do. The difficulty of travel leaves me, and many other visitors to Iran, at the mercy of a friend or a relative to take us to places we want to go. I have always had a nostalgic desire to find the kind, altruistic people who helped me so much when I was living in Iran. I fondly remember the tradesmen who offered me summer jobs simply because they wanted to assist me financially. I fondly remember the generous *bazaari* merchant who paid my first year of tuition, 850 *Tooman*, after I was accepted to Tehran University; I didn't have the money to enroll and was refused any kind of financial assistance. I also gratefully remember school teachers like Mr. Akbar Irani who gave their undivided attention to me and to other students, and spent hours and hours working with us to make sure that we received a good education.

On my last visit to Iran, I had to ask my nephew to take me to several places, especially to the burial ground where my parents rest. He was nice enough to help out despite his hectic work schedule. Visiting a graveyard can be a peaceful, reflective experience; however, it was not a pleasant one for me. I had a hard time not giving in to my rage when I found out that authorities had flattened the surface of the burial ground where my mother was buried and removed all of the tombstones. I felt that doing this was the utmost act of disrespect for those who were buried there and unable to raise objection because they were not alive. Sadly, even dead people are not respected and protected from the dehumanizing results of some government decisions in Iran. I wondered what kind of unsympathetic mindset could rationalize such an utterly disrespectful act. I was told that the only few graves that still remained intact were those belonging to VIPs who were members of the clergy. I couldn't comprehend what led the people who did this heartless act to believe that my mother, and the other innocent people who were buried there, were lesser beings than those few whose graves were preserved and protected.

Gravestones are the property of individuals. In addition, these personal markers have sentimental as well as historical value to relatives. In cases such as mine, gravestones are the only remaining evidence that a beloved deceased person existed. In light of this, the state should make laws to protect these markers against vandalism and illegal removal. The state must establish regulations concerning the removal of gravestones and unambiguously specify the circumstances under which they can be removed. Should circumstances dictate that gravestone removal is absolutely necessary, I believe this should be done with the knowledge of government officials but, more importantly, with the consent or at least advance proper notification of the relatives of the deceased. Arbitrary removal creates distrust of the government that is charged with protecting and the guaranteeing the private properties, rights, and dignity of citizens. Even if circumstances warrant removal of private property, the state must assume responsibility for the safe removal and preservation of the stones.

I was even more heartbroken after I realized that a gazebo-like room had been built on the very spot where my father and a few others were buried. This room was occupied by a couple of plain clothes guards who supposedly were in charge of maintaining order and holding the items that visitors were not allowed to carry inside the holy shrine. The desk they used for official business was placed directly on top of my father's grave. Under this dingy metal desk, I could see my father's tombstone with his named carved into it. The writing on the stone was barely readable because it was covered with dust and cigarette butts. I asked the guards if they would move their desk to the side so I could reach the gravestone. I wanted to clean it and touch it while praying for my father by reciting the opening Surah of Koran, *Fatehtol Ketab.* The Quranic prayer *Fateha,* is one of the Shia rituals allowing Muslims to pray for the soul of a deceased person. Washing and sweeping the dust off of a tombstone is also a customary way to pay tribute to the dead. The guards said there was no need for them to move their desk, and I could just pray standing up or even from outside of the room. I was tempted to remove the desk by force but I thought to myself, "Hey, who the hell are you, an obscure lecture reviser, to mess around with public officials; and why are you so fanatic about revering dead people in a society in which even those who are alive do not get much respect?" The situation was very tense but I did not allow my emotions to overpower my wisdom. I was able to restrain myself from arguing further because I thought it would be like trying to carry water in a strainer. I finally decided to leave the room and pray for my father outside. I left that place wondering how individuals who claim to be passionate guardians of the poor could be so insensitive and rude.

It is unbelievable to see how things have changed in Iran, leaving it so different now compared to the time when I lived there. Iranian cities have sprawled both quantitatively and qualitatively during the last two decades. My old friends are either dead, or have somehow disappeared, or are too lazy to get out of their houses. After so many years of living abroad, you feel like a stranger in your own home country. Much to my chagrin, everyone in Iran assumes that you are a *Haji Agha,* a title given to a person after they have completed a pilgrimage to Mecca. When I lived in Iran, being a Haji was a very rare and esteemed male-specific distinction. You could hardly find more than one Haji in one family. Today almost everyone, regardless of gender and age, is Haji. There is no longer any status or prestige attached to being a Haji. Hajis are like oversupplied commodities; they are everywhere. Anytime I went to a store, or anywhere else, I was addressed as *Haji,* as other men were, by default.

When shopping, I was really careful not to give any clues that might indicate I lived in the United States. If I did not exercise this care, I ran the risk of being overcharged by merchants, taxi drivers, flower shops, etc. However, there are certain words that we habitually keep repeating (dollar, post office, airport, passport, or referring to streets by their pre-revolution names) that give away the secret that we don't want the sales people to know. I remember once I asked a salesman, "Can you give me some sort of discount?" and he replied, "Do you bargain for lower prices in America too?" I had no idea how he found out that I lived in the United States. I pledged to myself that the next time I was in a store, I would be more cautious and not say anything dumb or commit any more stupid linguistic mistakes. Nevertheless, even with the pledge I made to myself still in the back of my mind, one day when I was in a clothing store looking for pants for myself, the salesman asked me the size of my waist and I said 32 inches! (they use the Metric system in Iran)

I remember from those days when I lived in Iran that life had its own built-in music. We woke up in the morning to the shouting of *Adasi* (cooked lentils) salesman; what an aromatic essence and yummy taste. After that there was the calling of other street vendors who would appear one after another; there was the vegetable seller, the ice cream man, the *laboo* (cooked beets) sellers, the *ab hosi (someone who empty the dirty water out of hous's pond)*, peddlers who sharpened knives and scissors, and the *chini band zan* (china dishes repair man). Even the squeaking noises of the horse-drawn carts (*Gaary*) had their own soothing rhythmic sounds. At night there were the irksome sounds of frogs, crickets, and other insects that, like the top officials of the Shah's regime, could always be heard but never be seen!

The Passage

I invite you to glimpse the "bridge time" that connected my journey from the "Misery Valley" of Iran to the "Missouri Valley" of the United States. It was not an easy bridge to cross. At times it was rough, uneven, and painful; at other times it was smooth, exhilarating, and led to possibility. In the end, in some ways I never want to completely make the crossing. I will forever have a part of my heart in Iran and my native culture, and a part of my heart in my new country.

I was quite young and full of joy and pride when I graduated from Tehran University, the only major state university in Iran, because my long held dream had come true. Back then in Iran, just being accepted as a college student was considered quite an accomplishment, but successfully sticking with it right through graduation was even more of an accomplishment. This was especially true for me because I was the first one in my family to go to college or have any kind of formal education for that matter. I had just turned 21 years of age at the time of my graduation, and was perhaps one of the youngest members of the class 1347-8 according to the Iranian calendar. Attaining a college degree in economics, which in those days was an exciting new and popular field of study, meant that the obvious source of a job for me was in government. In Iran, most of the jobs were and still are in government service. After enduring the convoluted hiring process, I was offered a job at the Department of the Interior. My apprehensive attitude toward government, which was a typical attitude among college students, did not make this job a good fit for me; however, I had no other choice but to accept it. After a few months of training I was sent to one of the northwestern provinces to work in a very small town as the assistant to the city governor. The main task of everyone in that office was to act as watchdogs for the government, or to put it more mildly, to act as public relations agents. One of our tasks was to listen to the complaints of the people about government officials, and to try to fulfill their requests to fix or improve social services. I still feel sorry for those people, especially the ones who had to travel all the way from remote rural areas to the city so they could voice their complains or concerns; they came thinking that we were their saviors. Truth be told, all we did was forward their requests to the "proper government authorities" for investigation, but in reality all that resulted was further delay, evasion, and more complications. Basically our main task was to organize and to supervise the so-called elections which were very corrupt processes. I remember in one local election on the night before the voting day, we were told to stuff the ballot boxes with phony ballots for the hand-picked candidate. The boxes then were to be transported to the election polling sites the next morning where the unsuspecting voters would cast their ballots not realizing the election had already been determined. That was the Shah's brand of a fair and honest voting process. I remember vividly that there was a man, Mashdi (Mr.) Abdullah, who was the full-time custodian of the building I worked in; he also served hot tea non-stop to the employees. One of the employees who were helping us with the phony ballots suggested teasingly that we cast a number of votes for Mr. Abdulla just for fun; we happily followed his suggestion. But when I returned home that night, it suddenly dawned on me about what could happen if the chosen candidate suddenly died in the night of natural causes or was killed in a traffic accident. Should something like this happen, Mr. Abdulla would be the next person in line because he would have the majority of votes. This heretofore unknown person would suddenly be thrust into power and the limelight, become a politician, and a member of the city council because of our fake votes. The thought of having no more hot tea provided for those of us who were left at the office was unimaginable. What was also unimaginable was the thought of having to endure the wrath of the powers that be that controlled the election.

For a person like me who used to keep a poster of Che Guevara in his room while a student, coping with the corruption and archaic ideas that were so prevalent in government offices was next to impossible. Also, since I was so young no one took me or my opinions seriously. I was like a mismatched patch on the intricate quilt of corrupt government employees. I was summarily dismissed as an idealistic, naive young boy who had nothing worthwhile to say or to contribute. No one took me seriously except for some of the local influential people who had marriage-age daughters hunting for a nice-looking, articulate son-in-law. Drum roll please! Marriage in our culture was, and still is, a family affair. These people who showed any interest in me were all wealthy, elitist Khans who were not at all compatible with my downtrodden family. Even if I intended to marry, which I didn't at that age, I would have been very careful not to marry anyone who would look down on and want me to reject my own family in any way.

The town in which I worked was small but modern; it had one major street which was also the walking track for our evening work out. We had nothing to do after the office was closed so we would walk up and down the street; we did this not only to get our physical exercise, but also to enjoy the clean serene weather. I remember I use to walk with a very articulate and opinionated friend of mine who also happened to be the only attorney in town. We usually discussed politics, especially the ongoing tensions between the Palestinians and Israel which was an emotionally charged issue even back then. We discussed how Mr. Anwar Sadat, the late president of Egypt and a close alley of the late

Shah of Iran, was handling the situation so cleverly! Almost every evening, we would eventually end up in the lobby of the only modern hotel built by the government. It was built mainly to accommodate the tourists because the town was on our country's border with Turkey, and a great number of Western tourists passed through it every day. No one dared to question or undermine the preeminence of Western tourists in Iran. Our parliament, yielding to the pressure exerted by the Shah, had passed the Capitulation Law which gave legal immunity to Westerners living or traveling in Iran.

All in all I considered my life as a government employee wasteful and unfulfilling, and wished to do something more honest, meaningful and constructive. I could not tolerate the ongoing corruption; no one could imagine how profoundly corrupt things were in the country unless he or she was on the inside, or was a part of it. Corruption on every level was a ubiquitous phenomenon in government offices in Iran. From the beginning of my employment at the Ministry of the Interior, I was always contemplating a way out. I knew I had to think about reorienting my career or else I would become contaminated by the culture of sleaze that was all around me. I finally decided to go back to school for graduate study. A few months back, a couple of my friends had already gone to the United States for the same reasons. I was in constant contact with them, and this fueled my strong inclination to also go to the U.S. to continue my education.

Obtaining a student visa from the U.S. embassy was very easy in those days because Iran, of all the countries in the Middle East, was its most loyal ally. Iran's U.S. installed government was largely controlled by U.S. officials. Our Shah was their Shah! In addition, the exchange rate between the U.S. dollar and Rial (the Iranian unit of currency) was reasonable and indeed affordable. An English translation of the official transcript of my undergraduate courses was the only document I needed to apply for admission to an American university. Many of the American universities, as well as the language schools, had their fully-authorized agents in Tehran. Many of these agents were endowed with a number of copies of prepared and, I believed, pre-signed I-20 forms—the official acceptance form to a U.S. university. I was able to obtain two I-20s within a few weeks; one was for admission to a university, and the other was for admission to an official English language school called ELS (English Language Services). I have no statistics to back it up, but based on my observations and popular opinion, Iran was the country with the largest number of foreign students studying in the U.S. in the early 70s. I could never have imagined in my wildest dreams that one day I would be able to travel to the U.S. for graduate study.

At long last the day for my departure had arrived. I had finally prepared all the needed documents and was able to buy all the airline tickets I needed to fly to the U.S. Overwhelmed by my exuberance over going to the U.S., I left Iran without even notifying my employer. If the Shah's regime was still in power today, I would still be an official government employee, or at least the beneficiary of my pension funds which consisted of a few hundred dollars that I contributed during the short period of my employment. At the time of my departure my monthly ending salary was 15,000 Rials which was equivalent to $200 in U.S. currency using the exchange rate that was in effect at the time. This was not bad for a single person considering the cost of living at that time. Fortunately I was able to have saved most of it. Thus, when I left Iran I had more than $2,100 to use as my start up money.

I finally arrived in Norman, Oklahoma, my final destination in U.S. It was a cold December day after a long journey that lasted for more than twenty four hours with frequent stops including the last one in Tulsa, Oklahoma. I complied with the requirement to report to the English Language Services school immediately upon my arrival. The school was located on one of the top floors of a huge dormitory building on the campus of Oklahoma University. I took the elevator to the floor where the school was located. There was nobody there because it was after hours and the school was closed. I was stranded on that floor with my bewilderment and my two pieces of luggage; I didn't know what to do other than wait. Fortunately, as I came to realize later, many of the students of that English school were Iranians who were living on that same floor. Luckily, I came across a couple of them who happened to be talking to each other in Farsi. I told them my story and was able to earn their sympathy after I sought their assistance. They informed me that the room next to their room was empty. It was connected to their room because both rooms shared one bathroom. I practically begged them to let me get into the room and sleep just for the night. They reluctantly agreed. Between you and me, this arrangement continued and I used that room free of charge for about a couple of weeks until I finally found three other Iranians students who were willing to share a rented apartment with me. What else could a frantic, moneyless man do? I considered this, my very first experience in the U.S., as a financial success thanks to my rigorous economic training! It gave credence to the expression that "necessity is the mother of all invention." I finally moved out of my unlawfully-occupied room into a fully furnished apartment.

For foreign students in those days, obtaining certain jobs was not difficult; almost everyone I knew worked in some capacity. However, foreign students were not permitted under immigration laws to work outside of the campus, but no one cared. We benefited fully from the lack of official government oversight. I started my first job in a restaurant as a car hop. It was fun and rewarding; in addition to an hourly wage, I received a lot of nice tips. Later on I found an ad in a local newspaper seeking truck drivers. I applied and was told that I had to have a valid commercial driving license. This did not present a problem for me. I was able to obtain an official truck drivers license the next day without paying a penny in bribes—sorry Mr. George Ryan—and started my new, adventurous job. The job was only one or two days per week, but the hourly pay was more than twice the minimum wage. So, I was the envy of the other students especially those who worked for the minimum wage. Driving a truck, albeit not a very long one, and delivering furniture to stores in different towns in the state of Oklahoma was really fun. It was like a paid vacation for me. After I delivered the furniture, I had to return the empty truck to a designated station. I remember the first day on the job was very hectic and action-packed. It was early in the evening; I was returning to Oklahoma City to return the truck when it suddenly stopped in the middle of the highway because it was out of gas. I pulled to the side of the road and desperately signaled the other drivers for help. After a few minutes a truck stopped; the driver got out and inquired about my problem. I explained that the truck had run out of gas. He then proceeded to tell me about the truck's spare gas tank which I was totally unaware of, and showed me how to switch it on. I followed his directions, started the truck, and returned to the station safe and sound. That was my first upsetting truck driving story but luckily it had a happy ending.

The number of temporary odd jobs I held during my student years is probably greater than the number of times Alex Rodriquez has been injected with steroids! Once I worked as a pizza deliverer which was an oddly eventful job. You never knew what kind of individuals you might end up encountering when delivering the pizza. Would you meet an intimidating redneck, a penniless student, a Ted Kaczynski-type loner, someone who whines for late delivery, a generous tipper? Even now I think about that job when I see that caveman in the GEICO commercials, or that lady from another commercial who always shows up at the door in her completely open night gown where one can see all too well that she is wearing nothing at all underneath, showing a the part of her body named in a theatrical monologue! She apathetically acted as if she was fully clothed. To this day, I still have no clue why anyone would ever do something like that.

The pizza store I used to work at was strategically located at the focal point in the campus corner. Even though the owner was a Jew, he was a nice man who was also very helpful and surprisingly generous toward the delivery personnel who were mostly of Middle East origin. The hourly pay, the tips, and the gas money made it a high paying job for recession-stricken students like me. The owner knew almost all of his customers and how much of a tip each customer would give; he tended to be fair in giving all of us as many tip-paying customers as possible. However, the highest tip orders usually were given to his favorite deliverer who regrettably was not me.

I never worked so hard in my life as I tried to balance my education with work. Also, who could resist the time consuming fun of the weekends? Most Saturday nights we use to go to a nightclub close to campus; its slogan was "if nudity offends you, do not enter here." We were all young, virile, and apparently not offended by nudity. We did not have much difficulty attracting nice or naughty girls! We always capitalized on our Middle Eastern complexions, and stroked ourselves with an assurance that some American girls had a distinct taste for men like us because we looked cutely different. I can't forget a horrific experience I had on one of those nights. A Native American Indian girl we kind of knew asked me for a ride back home and I agreed. I was about half way through the drive when I realized she lived in a remote rural area in another town. I had no choice but to continue to take her there. It turned out that it was her older sister's house. It was very late at night so her sister asked me if I wanted to sleep over and return home in the morning. I thought that was a wise idea because I didn't feel safe driving back late at night. After a couple of hours I woke up in the middle of the night to use the bathroom; that's when I found myself in a house full of Indian men sleeping everywhere, on the floor, on the couch, everywhere! I was relatively new to this country and didn't know much about Native American Indians except what we read in history books back home. I was so scared; I thought something dreadful might happen to me if I went back to bed. I was thinking about my folks back home and the fact that if something did happen to me under such circumstances no one would ever learn about it because the house was in the middle of nowhere. I thought a clever demagoguery was the only way out. So, I said politely and quietly to the lady of the house that I wanted to leave because I had to go to work early in the morning.

She said that she understood and gave me directions on how to find my way to the nearest town. I got out of the house, hopped into my car, started the engine, and drove away on the only dirty road leading away from this house. By this time it was about two or three hours passed midnight. I have never felt so frantic and frightened in my life. I drove aimlessly for awhile because I had no idea where I was going. It was a miracle that after a time I could see some lights indicating that there was a little town ahead. I drove toward the lights and eventually I arrived at three o'clock in the morning in a completely dead-asleep town. I stopped in an empty parking lot of a grocery store to check the only GPS I had in those days in my car, my AAA road map. My presence in that town that late at night was as unusual as the presence of a sexy bikini-wearing super model in the office of an ayatollah inquiring about religious matters. Thankfully a policeman showed up out of nowhere and inquired about what I was doing in this town and parking lot that late at night. I told him the story of my stupidity. He told me to follow his car until we reached the main highway that would take me back to Oklahoma City. It was like a mountain was being lifted off my chest. When I finally arrived back at the dormitory it was about sunrise. No one could believe my story or the extent of my foolishness. Because that was such an awful experience, I still remember its every detail. It is as if the picture of all those Indian men sleeping irregularly on the floor has been indelibly ingrained in my mind.

The most pleasant off-campus job I had was working in a restaurant which was in the lobby of the Holiday Inn in our town. The new owner, Mr. Tobin had just taken it over and he hired a few of us Middle Eastern students. We used to run the entire restaurant as a team. With the exception of the chef, the rest of the workers were Iranians. Mr. Tobin was so pleased with us; he kept telling us how much he had saved since we came to work at the restaurant. We were, indeed, careful to operate the restaurant as efficiently as possible using the business concepts we had learned at school. We were very careful not to waste, as our predecessors had, the expensive food materials. I was in charge of the salad bar before opening time; I was a waiter during opening time; and I was the cleaning man after closing time. Mr. Tobin's wife used to work as a waitress and she was a generous lady. She would stuff the money she received in tips into our pockets which was a nice gesture that strengthened our supportive attitudes. Her older sister also came to the restaurant everyday and worked even though she was in her early 70s. I liked her so much. She treated me as if I was her son, and in fact, she wanted to adopt me as her own son. I was hesitant to agree to do this because I thought doing so would be disrespectful to my own mother.

After I completed my master's degree work, I entered a doctoral program. I was awarded a scholarship after a couple of semesters that not only lowered my tuition costs, but also paid enough money for me to support myself. In the doctoral program I was enrolled in, nearly all were foreign students, mostly Iranians, and only a couple of students were American. We were all treated very nicely by our professors, others at the school in general, and in the economics department in particular. What else can you expect from an academic environment? It was in the job market that we felt the pinch of differential treatment, mistrust, and overt or covert discriminations, something that is even experienced to this day.

It was on a cold winter day when I finally departed Tehran for New York City on a TWA flight that ultimately ended in Norman, Oklahoma. I would spend about a decade of my life earning my master's and doctoral degrees. It wasn't easy to convince my mother that I planned to go to the US to study, but to lessen the hard reality for both of us I promised to write her a letter as frequently as I could. And I did. I still can see her standing next to the door, leaning against the wall, and trying to make sure that I was hearing her last motherly advice to me; she told me not to lose my faith and not to abandon my daily prayers. She also administered for me the Muslim ritual of walking three times under a copy of the holy Quran, and kissing it before I left the house to enter the waiting car that would take me to Tehran's only international airport. I still wish that I could know what was going through her mind at that very emotional moment as I was getting into the car and leaving her for an undetermined length of time. But what remained in my heart and mind was her one last request "Write me a letter as often as you can."

Regrettably my mother passed away a few years after I arrived in the U.S. At that time my daughter, my first child, was seven months old. The most concrete thing my mother had of her only American-born grandchild was a picture of her granddaughter which I had sent to her a few weeks after my baby girl was born. The last time I spoke to my mother, she took the opportunity to remind me of how much my daughter resembled her. She also told me that she was keeping that picture in her pocket all the time hoping that some day she would be able to hug her new granddaughter. Heartbreakingly for each of us, that day never came.

In his famous poem, Molana Rumi best describes the pain of past memories and the suffering that results from painful separations. In his most famous poem, a tale is told of a reed that has been cut from its root and is transformed into a lifeless musical instrument, a reed pipe. Anytime someone blows into the reed pipe, the reed breathes again, remembers its beginning, its home, reed-bed (*Naystan*), and its memories. Tired of feeling lonely and homesick, the reed starts groaning and telling stories about its home, *Nayastan*, the only place it knows as its home, the place in which it was born and raised. Through its musical sounds, the reed speaks about its sweet and bitter memories, remembers them with joy and regret, and describes the pain of separation.

Like the reed pipe of Rumi's tale, we too once were complete beings with a life full of hope, keen compassion, eagerness, anxiousness, and enthusiasm. Now, because of the passage of time, change and the decisions we have made in our lives, we too may find ourselves detached from our source, our roots; perhaps we may even have forgotten who we once were and where we came from. The bittersweet music of the reed with its intermingled tones of joy, regret and pain, speaks to us and to our hearts. The bittersweet music of the reed mirrors our own lives and serves as a reminder of our own past.

As I am sitting here in this house and living in this great country, I can't help but think of those formative early days that began and nurtured the story of my life. My life started humbly as I have described, and I believe in my heart of hearts that the events of my past and the people who were a part of my life were blessings that guided me toward the path that brought me to this part of the world and the life I now lead.

*   *   *

Like many other kids back home, I had to endure a variety of hardships in order to continue my education from one stage to the next. However, I can't keep myself from continuing to think about the many other kids in my neighborhood who were much more talented and much more eager than me to go to school and learn, but didn't have the opportunity. I hope this story is worthy of being dedicated to those kids. When I think of them, I sadly see them as beautiful flowers planted in a barren desert, growing up in obscurity, living lives of quiet desperation and eventually perishing in vain.

My Very First Bus Ride

In my elementary school, there were many students whose families could not afford to own an automobile so they did not have the opportunity to ride in one. Unluckily, I was one of them. For kids like me, riding in a car was a luxury that existed only in our dreams and we could only hope that one day those dreams might become reality. The very few kids whose families had an automobile, often made the rest of us envious by telling us stories about the pleasure of their joyrides. In those days, especially in small cities, one did not see Paykans, Peugeots, Patrols, or Prides, the automobiles that were popular in Iran. Horse-driven carriages served as the primary means of public transportation and the carriages pulled by two horses were considered to be deluxe models. Local bus service came to our town after I graduated from elementary school. I heard a story about one of our neighbors who, when he rode a service bus for the first time, gave a couple of fresh eggs to the driver as he was getting off the bus. The eggs were payment for his fare; one egg was for the driver and one egg was for the driver's wife who was referred to as *motealleghe,* my property! Don't get the wrong idea; it wasn't a barter system. It was just that some older people preferred to do things the old-fashioned way.

We used to run behind a speeding carriage until we could grab the metal rods on the top of the rear wheels; we would then jump up and sit on the back of the carriage for a free ride. It was cheap fun plus it also got us from one place to another for free. It was even more enjoyable to share the illegal ride with a friend, given that the back-end of the carriage was wide enough to accommodate two passengers. However, often the joy was very short-lived. Sometimes the ride ended painfully when the carriage-driver *(soorchi)* became aware of us and either stopped the carriage to get rid of us or forced us to get off using strokes of his lash. Once, a rumor circulated at our school that even Mr. Khatib, the youngest teacher who was recently hired, would sometimes ride on the back of a carriage to get to school on time! We felt vindicated when we heard that rumor because it made us feel better about our mischievous behavior.

I also vividly remember when I rode a bus for the first time. My parents decided to take me to Teheran to visit some relatives *(sele arham),* not for pleasure but as a recommended religious duty. Pleasure trips were as scarce for us as a copper bowl in a bear's house, *khneh kherse va badieh mess?* We spent a long time in the waiting area of the only major bus station in our town; the station was called "Garage Transport." Whether we liked it or not, we had to wait until there were enough passengers to fill all the seats in the bus. Eventually the waiting was over. It felt like God gave me the whole world when the assistant driver told us we could get on the bus. I was so excited I jumped up and down like a monkey. My life long dream was about to become a reality. I was the first to get on the bus.

Kids didn't receive much attention and were considered to be parasites (*tofaili*). As such, my parents didn't even think about buying a ticket for me, so consequently, I had no seat. I decided that I would like to sit on the VIP bucket chair in the first row next to the driver's seat. It would be delightful for me to watch the outside scenes through the huge front window of the bus. I would fully enjoy my temporary self-bestowed opportunity. Ultimately, where I would sit depended on the mercy of the assistant driver. If there were not enough passengers to fill the entire bus, he may offer me a regular seat, or at least, a stool to sit on. Unfortunately, I was not even offered that; instead I crawled up and down in the middle alleyway between the rows of seats. I was like a homeless person who was unsuccessfully searching for a place to settle down. A passenger, who was probably trying to alleviate my suffering, offered me a piece of candy called *noghl shekar panir*. An older couple sitting in the next row gave me a piece of home-made bread and a chunk of white goat cheese and insisted that I eat. They were telling me in their cute Turkish language, "Eat; they are very delicious (*chokh yemali deer*)."

Unlike the contemporary buses of today, the buses in those days were not equipped with safety features or comforting amenities. The buses were very basic and were shaped like a huge, tall Zamboni with a long nose. They were noisy, rattled and trembled, especially when they were going fast. The bus we were on was a very close approximation of the machine of *Mashdi Mamd Ali*. Stubborn like a mulish mule, it seemed that the bus was not willing to carry any passenger anywhere. After spending some time on the road to Tehran, the bus started tossing us, especially those sitting in the back rows, up and down. I imagined that maybe because of its big nose, the bus was sneezing too often. When we got to Ali Abad, almost half way to Tehran, many of the passengers had already thrown up. One could tell what a person had for lunch from the smell of their vomit! By this time, the bus was filled with all kinds of terrible odors and I was about to throw up. Luckily, the driver stopped the bus in front of a road-side tea house so the passengers could get a much needed rest; *ab chopogh,* as he told us. The passengers, who were tired and had a dire need to use the bathroom, did not exit the bus in an orderly fashion. The assistant driver made it clear that everyone should return to the bus in about 45 minutes. It was, I believe, beneath the dignity of the bus driver to explain any details to the passengers; this duty was left to his assistant.

Many times when the bus struggled to climb up hills or to make sharp turns on that dangerous road to Tehran, the panicking travelers prayed and recited *salavat*, especially for the safety of the bus driver, Aghye Ronandeh. I guess others didn't deserve that kind of blessing. Be that as it may, we continually prayed for the driver's safety in an effort to insure that he got us to our destination safe and sound. If people's deeds in this world are the basis for the decision on judgment day as to whether they go to heaven or to hell, I think Iranian bus drivers will all get into heaven because the way they drive turns everyone on their buses into pious prayers!

After a short rest in the tea house, the assistant driver announced loudly that all passengers must return to the bus. Gradually, we all entered the bus and patiently waited for the driver to return. It seemed like the bus driver felt it would be demeaning for him to return to the bus before all of the passengers; therefore, he had to be the last to get in.

We were about to "start counting down for the take off" when we noticed that one of the passengers, Amoo Gholi, was missing. He was an old man, probably in his early sixties, who was retired not because he was too old to work, but because he was physically too frail to do any manual labor. Like other older men, Amoo Gholi was at the mercy of his sons, especially the eldest son who traditionally was obligated to take care of his aging parents. His wrinkled pale face was indicative of lifelong hard work in hot, sunny weather as well as malnutrition and inadequate healthcare services. He reminded me of the tale of the bitter bird who lives in the reedy marshes and does nothing but endure grief. It was so sad to see men like Amoo Gholi whose physical and mental capacities have been depreciated due to decades of hard work serving society. Now that he was old and unable to support himself, society had turned its back on him, assumed no responsibility for him, and left him to the mercy of his sons who could hardly provide for their own families.

We searched and searched, but found no trace of Amoo Gholi. It seemed, as Americans would say, he either turned into smoke and vanished into thin air, or turned into water and penetrated the ground. A few of the passengers searched every corner of the tea house to no avail. They even knocked on every door in the men's restrooms. They didn't hear the sound of Amoo Gholi's *ehen!*

In the meantime, the hot temperature inside the bus made waiting more unbearable for most of the passengers and they started to voice their complaints. Everyone tried desperately to find a solution to this dilemma. The number of recommended solutions was very small and some of them were either strange or impractical. At last, after much deliberation, we concluded that Mr. Amoo Gholi must have inadvertently gotten on a wrong bus and who knows where he is now. The passengers agreed that further waiting was useless and the journey should continue without him. However, no one had the courage to say this to Mr. Gholi's eldest son who was one of the passengers and supposedly in charge of him.

Illustrating the saying that necessity is the mother of all practical inventions and adversity is the source of creativity, one of the passengers suddenly made a strange suggestion. "Why don't we look inside that bus that is parked at the far corner of the tea house's yard?" he yelled. The bus he was referring to was disabled, abandoned, and left at that spot until it would be transported to a junkyard. Many who had been helplessly inactive until that moment suddenly jumped up voluntarily and ran toward the abandoned bus. Surprisingly, it was an accurate guess. Amoo Gholi was in that bus and had been waiting and wondering where the hell the other passengers were!

When the anxious searchers entered the abandoned bus, they saw Amoo Gholi lying down relaxingly on a seat like a soldier who is assured of permanent peace. He was praying and reciting *ayatal korsi* for the safety and happiness of all believers, particularly his fellow passengers. When Amoo Gholi saw the searchers, he started yelling, asking them why they had kept him waiting and where they had been. In other words, Amoo Gholi, the source of all the problems, now considered himself a victim and accused us of carelessness and procrastination. I think many of us may behave exactly like this in real life when we create problems for others by our sloppy actions or hasty decisions. All too often, such decisions, which we may consider trivial, not only do not solve any problems but may even create new ones.

Finally, Amoo Gholi was transferred to our bus with full ceremony and we continued our journey. Many passengers did not hesitate to show their anger by scolding the poor old man mercilessly for the mistake he made unintentionally. I, however, didn't think they had a right to do that. The fact that some people like Amoo Gholi may be absent-minded or naïve should not give us an excuse to blame them for an accidental mistake. We have to accept the fact that people are different, physically and mentally and many may not be as clever as we are. We should like every person for the way he or she is and not for the way we think he or she should be.

How I Became My Older Brother

"I am sure this is a problem that hopefully can be rectified," said my sixth grade teacher. While he was patting my back gently as the sign of support, he told me, "You should be able to take the final exams when we correct the mistake."

After nearly fifty nine years of age, I still think about my boyhood memories and cherish them with an open heart. Maybe the weird and wonderful stories that happened in my life in the very distant past are reawakening my mind to my childhood years. Past memories appear like crystal clear drops of water providing me with interesting subjects to write about. They are like burning clean natural gas, creating clear blue flames; they are like acid reflux at the middle of night keeping me awake and thinking.

A few months ago when I traveled to Iran and stayed for a few weeks, I visited my hometown, a place I left a long time ago. Because of mushrooming sprawl, I could hardly find my way and barely recognized the old streets. The population explosion was evident everywhere. Where did all these people come from?

A few weeks ago, I finished reading a book in which there was a story about an old Palestinian Muslim man named Abdullah Kadooreh. He is over 100 years old and has 240 sons, daughters, grandsons and grand daughters. One of my own relatives, who passed away a few years ago in Iran, was survived by seven sons, two daughters and nearly 45 grandsons and granddaughters. In western countries it is quite the opposite; a typical old man may have only one or two children and a few grand children. According to some projections, if the current population growth rate in Muslim countries continues into the future, soon there will be more Muslims in the world than there will be Christians. One projection estimates that the world population will be 30 percent Muslim and 25 percent Christian by the year 2025. One can draw one's own conclusion regarding this demographic trend, however, some observers see this as a troubling concern.

After walking through the streets of my hometown for a while and with the help of an old friend who functioned as my tour guide, I was able to find my parents' house, the house in which I was born and grew up. The house was sold many years ago, so I had to negotiate with the new owner who finally gave us permission for a visit. Even though all sections of the house were the same as they had been in my youth, my first impression was that they looked a lot smaller than what I had imagined in my mind. The width and the length of the alleys around our house also seemed shorter. I thought to myself that perhaps living in the United States for so long had given me inflated expectations and the impression that everything must be big. The only good thing about this house when we lived in it was that it had a natural immunity to thievery and vandalism. As a result, our house didn't need any security systems to ward off potential burglars or even a solid entry door to discourage break-ins by thieves hoping to steal money and other valuables. Finding a needle in a haystack would have been easier than finding anything worth steeling in our house because it was completely built from mud bricks with no single piece of brick in its structure. Our house always reinforced the feeling inside of me that we may have somehow fallen out of favor but we did not stop asking God for guidance and blessings everyday. If nature (God) was fair to us, why was our house made out of mud and dirt? I use to utter to myself as a child (*agar zamaneh ba ma adel bood, chera khane ma as khesht o kel bood*).

Our house had two sections. One section was the place in which we lived. The other section, which was closer to the entrance, was the place where we kept domesticated animals such as cows, calves, occasionally sheep and a female donkey which functioned as our transportation system. A red crowned rooster (the alarm clock for us and for our neighbor) and the hens were allowed to roam anywhere throughout the house. I vividly remember when the roof of our house was soaked with rain water on hot summer days; the smell of mud was so exotically effervescent! It relieved us for a while from the odor of cow manure. The house had neither running water nor electricity. Finding things at night using the kerosene fueled lantern was not very easy nor was this effort uneventful. The basement of our house was a museum of completely useless antiquities. In those days, older people even saved their garbage in the hope that someday it might come in handy. The walls of our basement were the "theatre of operations" for pests, especially cockroaches, and its floor was the place where the hens laid their eggs.

On cold winter nights when the sub-zero wind slapped your face like the whipping of modern day morality enforcers, we all sat under the cozy and warm traditional *korsi* in what some in America might call the master bedroom. It was the bigger of the only two bedrooms in our house. My father entertained us with his mind-grabbing stories which made it easier for us to endure the boredom of such nights. Almost all of his stories ended with a fatherly advice for us kids. Since I was the youngest child (*tah taghari*), I had the privilege of sitting on my father's lap. He would sing songs for me that started with a phrase like, "You are so dear to my heart, my red flower." Such inspirational songs strengthened my sense of bonding and belonging. I listened to my father's stories so intently that often I woke up at the middle of the night thinking about the deprived life of *Hassan kachal*, the hero of most of his stories

I was born in that house. When, nobody knows. In those days, it was not important to uneducated people like my parents to record the exact date of their children's birth. I am not even sure to this day whether my conception was actually planned or had been the result of my father's compliance with the advice of the residing mullah of our mosque. The mullah told his audience that *nazdiki* (an implied term for sex) with your wife on Thursday night is *mostahab* (recommended) and is like killing one of the enemies of the imam's family! I don't even know whether my parents celebrated my birth. Frankly, I was perhaps viewed as an extra burden given their limited food supply and their other resources. I don't remember having a birthday party because obviously no one knew my exact date of birth. Even if they did know, I am not sure that anyone cared. We believed luxury amenities like birthday parties were only for upper class families and, therefore, not for us. Or maybe after raising six other children, my parents didn't have enough stamina for the seventh child. According to economic theory, the value of my existence was subject to the law of diminishing marginal utility; the more you have of something, the less valuable the additional unit becomes. I had no doubt that someone knew my exact birth date. Surely someone like the mullah, who recited *azan* and *eghame* (a religious ritual) In my right and left ears at my birth, must have recorded my birth date on the cover of the holy Koran. However, no one in my own family seemed to know if that happened.

Both of my parents were formally illiterate as were the other members of my family. People working in government offices did not want to deal with illiterate people and were unwilling to listen to their needs and concerns. The official businesses of such illiterate citizens, therefore, must be taken care of through middlemen known as *ghal chagh kon*, a literary term for liaison or lobbyist. Mr. Sar Khosh was the only such liaison operating in the area where we lived. Many years after my birth, my father finally recognized the necessity of obtaining an official identification document for me so I would have a formal declaration of my existence. In an attempt to help, Mr. Sar Khosh who was perhaps a kindhearted man, intentionally understated the age of the male children in order to postpone the occasion when they were summoned to compulsory military service. I learned later on that my father, following the instructions of Mr. Sar Khosh, agreed to understate my age when he applied for my birth certificate. This was not an unprecedented practice in those days.

Officially I did not exist until my birth certificate, *shenasnameh*, was issued, recorded, numbered, and sanctioned by the government. Frankly, there was no compelling reason for my father to obtain a birth certificate for me. The semi-primitive school I attended up until sixth grade required no formal identification document for registration and enrollment. It seemed that it operated under an honor system where the verbal information given by a parent or guardian was sufficient for enrollment. As graduation approached and I began preparing to take the required state-sponsored final exams, my secret was revealed; I was attending the school for many years illegally because I wasn't old enough.

For the first time in my life I had the opportunity to pose for a picture in front of a photographer's camera. The school-district officials needed my picture in order to issue me an entry permit for the final exams. The next day I showed up at school with my black and white pictures, my not-so-accurate birth certificate in my school bag and with great enthusiasm in my heart. It didn't take long for my excitement to turn into disappointment and my hope into despair. It was my teacher who informed me of the bad news; there was a big problem. I was not old enough to be legally eligible to take the final exams. My teacher, Mr. Irani, God bless his soul, said in disbelief, "You are even younger than my grandson! How can you take the sixth grade exams?" Taking the sixth grade graduation exams, for me an eight year old kid, was of course against the law. He told me that either there is a problem with my birth certificate or I must be extraordinarily ingenious to be able to finish elementary school at so young an age. Proving my ingenuity was difficult; therefore, he deduced that there must be a problem with my birth certificate. He didn't know that it was not a mistake but rather a deliberate misrepresentation by my parents who thought they were doing me a favor. He informed me that I had no choice; I had to become a twelve year old kid whatever the expense.

When they made the decision to fabricate my official age, neither my father nor Mr. Sar Khosh considered that I might go to school someday. All they were concerned about at the time was finding a legal loophole that would delay my military service. Military service was a hardship for poor Iranian families. My father could not even imagine in his dreams that one day his son might attend school. Who would have thought in those days, that the sons of a peasant would even go to elementary school let alone a university? The sons would be badly needed by the family to help with the extremely labor intensive farming activities.

I remember during the weekends, I had to go to my father's farm to help him and his partners with the chores. Understandably, the kids were not assigned the technical jobs such as cutting vegetables. Those tasks would only be done by adults because the adults feared that the kids might damage the roots of the vegetable plants if they were allowed to cut them. Our work was mainly peripheral and/or logistic, such as washing the vegetables, bunching them, and preparing them for market. The physical pressure of washing vegetables, especially green onions, in cold stream water was almost unbearable. When you were done, you could hardly stand up straight again.

Not to seek a solution would be a concession to defeat. There is a substitute available for almost everything we need. There should be, therefore, a workable substitute for my inaccurate official birth certificate as well. My six-grade teacher asked me curiously, "Do you have an older brother?" "Yes" I replied. His face suddenly brightened as a solution struck his mind like a thunder bolt. He suggested that the only way to solve the problem was to switch my birth certificate with my brother's. This was a no-cost, no fault, solution without any headaches, but more importantly, it required no assistance from any government agency. It is better for a person to be a dog than to be in need of government services in Iran. I had no choice but to accept his suggestion that I switch my birth certificate with the one belonging to my older brother. My teacher cautioned, however, that no one was to know about this covert tactical operation and the great identity swap must remain our secret forever. This decision made me feel a bit uneasy because it required that I assume my brother's name and use his other personal information after the exchange was done. Despite my unease, arrangements were made for me to become a new person. Fortunately, the school I attended was like ancient *maktabs*. There were no records, no transcripts and no portfolios. Everything was based on an honor system. In my childish innocent mind, I was afraid and had a feeling that if we went ahead with the identity switch plan, the law enforcement officials would raid our school and take the perpetrators of this crime to prison. Little did I know that such practices were, if fact, very routine in those days.

Eventually, my qualms about my teacher's suggestion began to dissipate. It sounded expedient and practical. Furthermore, that was the only way I could achieve my dream of graduating from elementary school and free myself from the entangled mess created by adults when I was born. My teacher told me to come back to school the next day with my father and with my older brother's official birth record.

The next morning, my father dressed up, put on his *dabit haj ali akbari's tomboon* which was like his formal pants, and accompanied me to school. He shook my teacher's hand using both of his hands. This was a respectful way for ordinary people to shake hands with someone who was really important to them. Then, he put his right hand on his heart; he bowed and stood up near the wall. In other words, the poor man honored all the ceremonial codes of respect that are expected only from those at the bottom of the social scale.

We triumphed! We solved the problem that could have cost me the successful completion of my sixth grade. I enrolled at my school again, this time under my older brother's name. I became a new person who was now older by a few years and more hopeful by a leap. From that day on, I attended the rest of the school year using my phony identity. I became my older brother and he unwillingly became me. It seems that the substitute identification has served me quite well so far. I am not unhappy with the way things have turned out for me but I want to apologize to those whose lives were in any way screwed up by this mishmash. And I wish to thank my older brother, an experienced mechanic living in Iran, who had no choice but to relinquish his birth certificate to me so that I could continue with my education. To this day, I believe, he has not been able to explain to his kids why their father and their uncle both have the same name!

Part II

Finding the Humor

Sir, Are You Iranian Too?

It was more than 35 years ago when I entered the United States for the first time on a non-stop flight from Tehran to New York City by Iran Air. It was the early 1970s, so I was not forced to take off my jacket, belt and shoes at the airport, or submit to a body search like people have to do today at airports. I carried a big brown suitcase in my right hand. It was full of stuff, including half a dozen hand-made shorts which were packed into the suitcase by my mother. Evidently my mother thought I was going to a "shortless" country! I also had an English-Persian dictionary in my left hand, $2,100 in my pocket, and a burning desire to succeed in my heart. The only other places I had traveled to before coming to the United States were Tehran and a couple of other Iranian cities. In the airport I was acting like a nincompoop, bewildered and baffled. Any observer could surmise from my behavior that I was not a seasoned traveler, however, I felt like someone who was dispatched to an unknown territory for a really important mission. Even though the main reason for coming to the

United States was the continuation of my education, I have to admit that curiosity was also a determining factor. I believe curiosity is a constructive attribute of the Iranian people who are renowned for seeking knowledge from cradle to grave! I believe that when you study in another country, you are stronger in your resolve to succeed and, therefore, have a greater chance of attaining better academic credentials.

You guessed correctly that things were much different in those days. Let me review for you some of the historical realities of that time. Richard Nixon was the President of the United States. The cold war was a hot topic. The expression "safe sex" had a totally different connotation than what it has today. Body piercing was not a way of expressing yourself. The Chevy Vega was the only compact fuel efficient American car. Cher was still married to Sonny. Adam Smith was famous and nobody knew the name Anna Nicole Smith. The hottest show on TV was *All in the Family*. Holidays were mostly *holy days*. The only famous Paris Hilton was the Hilton in Paris. There was no need to remind people to turn off their cell phones in public places. Obesity was not a troubling issue for this nation. The most likely reason for Monica Lewinsky to have to crawl under a desk would have been to find her missing toys! Punch card machines were the state of the art data processing apparatus. Crisco not Cisco was the rising star of Wall Street. You used a book and "let your fingers do the walking" when you wanted contact information. And most importantly, the rate of exchange between the U.S. dollar and *Rial* (Iranian currency) was about 1 to 75. It seems like the only thing that hasn't changed, at least as yet, is that kitchen cabinets still do come with a *Lazy Susan*!

Because of a lack of experience and/or sheer ignorance, we newcomers made serious mistakes. This chagrined those who came to this country before us because they thought they were superior to us. A few examples of things that annoyed them were: entering a store through the exit door or exiting through the entry door, eating food with a spoon in the school cafeteria instead of using a fork, reusing disposable cups and dishes, or the worst thing one could do, walk down the dormitory hallway in pajamas! All these were considered indefensible crimes that only naïve newcomers like me would commit.

Coming to the U.S. was really a big deal for me because I had never before been to any foreign country. I was very anxious but also somewhat excited at the same time. In my simplistic mind, I had a black and white image of America. I thought America was a huge land mainly occupied by houses and smoke-emitting factories. I thought most of its areas were brackish, dusty and arid land. I thought its population was comprised mostly of rough and unfriendly cowboys who had skewed attitudes toward foreigners. In the beginning of my sojourn in America, everything seemed odd and unusual due to my inadequate knowledge of the popular culture and the norms of its society. I was very careful not to engage in any embarrassing behavior. I did not want to do anything that could be indicative of my backwardness or be interpreted as a lack of respect for others. Inadequate knowledge of the popular culture of this country often resulted in misinterpretation of the behavior of others toward me. For example, if someone had a smile on his/her face when approaching me, I told myself that this person must like foreigners, especially me. I amused myself with the thought that I was indeed a very popular person. I did not even remotely think that American people could be naturally cheerful. Even if sad things happen to them, they don't lose their sense of restraint and humor. In other words, they take things easy.

At first I thought that this obvious difference between the American culture and the Iranian culture might create problems for me, but then I realized that there is no such thing as an exclusive American culture. America as a nation is an amalgam of different people who gradually migrated to this great land bringing their cultures with them. These diverse peoples and their cultures have become the varied patches in a beautiful, well designed national quilt—heterogeneous and full of colors. I had no choice but to become another piece of this magnificent quilt. I contributed to this magnificent quilt by assimilating into the American culture while also keeping and treasuring my own Iranian culture. However, this was not easy to accomplish; there were times in the process when I felt like I was a thick strand of thread being forced through the tiny hole of a needle.

My resistance weakened as I confronted and eventually gave in to the irresistible longing for hedonistic American culture. Soon, *aab* (Farsi word for water) was changed to water and *noon* (bread in Farsi) was changed to bread. I ate soup instead of *aash* and chicken broth instead of *abgoosht*. The word *salam* was changed to hello and the word *tonboon* (pants in Farsi) was changed to jeans. At the same time, however, nostalgia and feelings of homesickness continued to gnaw within me. I was losing my *Iranianness*! In an effort to fill the void created by loneliness, I constantly searched for things of my own Iranian culture that had traces of home. When I would see a person who resembled an Iranian, I would talk to myself loudly in Farsi, or I would whistle a famous Farsi tune hoping to capture the person's attention. However, given my bad luck, the person would turn out to be Mexican, Greek or Arab, leaving me disappointed. These people, some even more confused than I was, provided me with a little relief; they reminded me that I was not the only stranger in this country. Other techniques I employed to get the attention of Iranian look-alikes did not produce any tangible results either. However, the sad realization that it was really difficult to find other Iranians did not weaken my determination. I felt that it was neither feasible nor convenient to always associate informally only with Americans. I yearned to find a few Iranians, especially from my home town, to chat with and to talk about the native things we shared.

On a practical level, another looming concern was the fear that I would be forced into the vicious state of indigence if I ran out of money. Even though I was not supposed to work for money while I was on a student visa, I tried to find legal loopholes in immigration laws that would allow me to find legal and gainful employment. I also thought that working at a job could strengthen my English language skills, especially my conversional proficiency, because I would be dealing with people who spoke English.

I am pretty sure that the official minimum wage rate was $1.60 those days, equivalent to $7.45 at today's prices. When I multiplied this number by 75, it amounted to 120 Rials per hour or 960 Rials per day. I had been use to living on forty to fifty Rials per day back home; so for me, this was a huge amount of money and it gave me an additional motive to work. As they say, people respond to monetary incentives.

Back in those days, the best way to find a job was to read through the classified ads in local newspapers. Today one would use careerbuilder.com! Everyday I would check the local newspapers in our school's library hoping to find a decent, good-paying job. One day the following advertisement caught my attention: "Wanted, an energetic young man to work in a local zoo; English proficiency and experience are not necessary." It seemed to be an ideal position for me. I was young, energetic, without any work experience and, of course, I was not very proficient in English. I called to inquire about the job and was invited to come for an interview. When I went for the interview, I made my first embarrassing linguistic error when I told the secretary that I had a "date" with the manager. What I meant, of course, was that I had an appointment with the manager. I saw the belittling smile on her face as she guided me toward the manager's office. It turns out that the manger with whom I had a "date" was a muscular man with a thick mustache!

It didn't take long for me to discover that the job I was being interviewed for was an unbelievably odd one. It was explained to me with a great deal of sorrow that the only male lion in the zoo had passed away recently and zoo officials as yet had not been able to find a replacement. Finding a live replacement, I was told, required an extensive search which would take a long time. Therefore, the zoo officials had decided to hire a human replacement for the deceased male lion, someone who would slip into a lion costume and pretend to be a live lion! The position would be temporary until they found a real live lion. I thought they were playing a practical joke on me but they were desperately serious. At first I was kind of flattered when they told me that I was a perfect candidate for this job. However, I found out later on that they had not been able to find a viable candidate who had guts enough to become a fake lion. I told them I needed some time to think about their job offer.

After a brief consultation with myself where I weighed the costs and the benefits, I persuaded my left brain that it was not a terribly bad job for me. First, the hourly payment was above the minimum wage rate. Secondly, I did not have a boss ordering me around and telling me what to do. Thirdly, no one will ever find out that it was me disguised as a lion; the whole thing would remain a secret forever. Finally, it wasn't going to be my permanent job and in the meantime, I could use my resources to find a more reputable job. Reluctantly, I accepted the job and was told to show up for work early the next morning. The joyous reaction of my new employers to my acceptance was testimony to the extreme anxiety they felt in being unable to find a fool like me who would be willing to say yes to such a silly offer. The next morning I showed up on time to start my adventurous job. A few days went by without incident and the true personality of the fake lion remained concealed from the visitors. Thank God they were not allowed to feed the animals. In summary, the first act of this dramatic show was executed successfully.

One day, I was really tired because of inadequate sleep the night before. As a result while on duty, I fell into a very deep sleep similar to the afternoon nap taken by construction workers (*amaleh*) on a hot summer day back in Iran. During my sleep, I had a dreadful nightmare. I saw in my dream, while I was performing my daily routine as a fierce lion jumping up and down, two wild tigers approaching me from a not too far distance. Given that I was only a timid human being in the costume of a lion, I was so frightened that I was about to wet my pants. I tried to calm and console myself by reminding myself that the two approaching tigers don't know I am not a real lion. Theoretically, I was the king of the jungle and all the other animals should respect and be afraid of the king. On the other hand, I asked myself what would happen if they found out I was only a phony. Would I then become the main course of their afternoon meal? I started blaming myself for being stupid enough to take this job. I said to myself in Farsi the Farsi expression, "This was the soup I myself poured into my own bowl!" Now, my dream of getting a good education in the United States was about to be shattered. A docile person who had led a relatively pressure free life until now, was about to suffer the pressure of the powerful jaws of these wild tigers!

Strange thoughts such as these were scratching the surface of my brain like broken pieces of glass and raising my heart beat so swiftly that I suddenly woke up. I was greatly relieved because waking up was the best remedy for my misery, and I thanked God that I was finally free from that horrible nightmare. But then all of a sudden, I saw two real tigers a few yards away from me and I could see them with my own open eyes this time. This was not a dream any more; what I was seeing was real, actual not imaginary, factual not fictional. I said to myself that this was more bad luck and things couldn't get any worse. The two tigers were staring curiously at me; they seemed to be thinking about attacking me and I thought this was it. I am done, finished, gone, and should get ready for my final exit. I was about recite my *shahadatain* (religious testimony to the existence of God and the prophet Muhammad). Instead, by force of habit, I suddenly said as loudly as I could in Farsi, "*God*

Please save me" I am begging you. Much to my astonishment the two tigers suddenly burst out laughing and started talking in human voices. They asked me simultaneously in Farsi, "Sir, are you Iranian too?" I will never forget the immense joy I experienced in that moment, not because fate finally saved my life, but because I had found other Iranians at last!

Being Ignored

This piece is intended to be mainly humorous and entertaining. The following reflections on my being the target of subtle discrimination are not intended to promote or justify self-pity or whining. Self-pity is not a desirable attribute and we should stay away from it. I believe self-pity is a symptom of weakness that demonstrates one's inability to cope with challenging situations. A person who wallows in self-pity chooses to blame others for their failures instead of utilizing their personal strengths and resources to better their life. With my intention clarified, I would like to share some experiences and thoughts about being ignored.

I was returning home the other day on a commuter train when suddenly one of the passengers in the train car sneezed; many passengers reacted kindly by saying "God bless you." A few minutes later I sneezed, not once but twice, and no one said anything to me in blessing. After a while, I sneezed again intentionally so as to test my hypothesis that people were in fact ignoring me.

My hypothesis proved to be valid when, yet again, I received no reaction or blessing from the passengers around me. This showed me that even the thoughtful custom of saying "God bless you" after someone sneezes is not extended to minorities. This is how overtly minorities are being ignored by others in America! But I have become Very used to this kind of discrimination after so many years of having experienced it. Don't jump to a premature conclusion. No, I am not a timid, turned-off bore with geeky attitudes. It is just a sad reality that "being ignored" is one of the downsides of being a member of diaspora in this country. I believe that even if a disaster like a tornado hit my neighborhood, it too would ignore me and skip my house! Simply stated, minorities are not protected by the Equal Attention Opportunity laws! When I make contributions at a meeting or when working on a committee, my opinions are not usually taken seriously. However, if the same or similar views are expressed by others, they are applauded.

Oprah is not my most favorite TV show but I watch it occasionally simply because my favorite show, *Jerry Springer*, is aired at a time when I am usually at work. The last time I watched Oprah, the show featured a female guest and the title of the show was "Coming Out of the Closet." Until then, I did not know that coming out of a closet was such an enormous accomplishment that it bestowed the status of national celebrity on the person coming out of the closet. This is just another example of how much I am being ignored in this country. I have closets in every room of my house. I go into the closet and come out of the closet many times every day and no one, absolutely no one, cares! How much further can the problem of double standards extend?

I have suffered with AADS (Adult Attention Deficit Syndrome) for a long time and I have finally decided to do something to alleviate it. I have resorted to every conceivable tactic to get others to acknowledge my presence and give me some attention, often unsuccessfully. These tactics are not always effective because they are plainly silly. So, if silliness offends you, please skip the next few paragraphs and move right on to the last paragraph.

When I go to the grocery store for instance, I leave my shopping cart unattended hoping that someone will pick it up by mistake. When someone does take the cart by mistake, I approach him/her with a gracious greeting and proceed to reclaim my shopping cart, however, my hidden agenda is to start a conversation. At other times, I stand on the sidewalk in front of my house with a heavy duty 1600 watt hair dryer in my hand pointed at the approaching vehicles. I scare the drivers by pretending that I am a plain clothes law enforcement agent who is checking the speed of moving vehicles. My hope, however, is that at least some of them will stop and beg me for leniency. Of all the silly strategies I've tried, the one that has worked the best so far is when I go to the aerobics class in my fitness club and I suddenly, intentionally, fake a seizure in the middle of the exercise routines. I then pray that I will get lucky and a beautiful young lady will voluntarily give me mouth to mouth resuscitation. Other techniques that I have developed so meticulously have not been as effective as I hoped they would be. Some of these techniques include but are not limited to: requesting that my telephone be taken off the Do Not Call list, sending e-mail to myself, stopping payment on my bills in the hope that a collection agency would call me, going into an antique store and asking "What's new?" and going into a toy store and asking if they have a disposable boomerang! All these techniques, clever as they may be, have not resulted in satisfactory outcomes.

But the good news is that I am eventually becoming more popular as I get older, especially when it gets close to my birthday. Like you, I receive many letters of solicitation every day. Debt consolidators, bankruptcy lawyers, online dating service companies and particularly life insurance companies, have become compassionately interested in my welfare. They keep sending me thoughtfully written letters; however, they are usually addressed to Ms. or Mrs. Varjavand. What I don't understand is that if these people are so concerned about my welfare and the well being of my family, why don't they bother to find out whether I am male or female? One time I even received an invitation from a pageant organizing company to participate in the state beauty pageant! Apparently they must think not only that I am a lady but also that I am a very beautiful young lady! The invitation was serious and contained complete step-by-step instructions for preparation. They even promised to assist me in fund raising and forming a support committee of relatives, friends and other volunteers.

And to you annoying junk e-mailers and modern e-stalkers who pretend to care about me unselfishly, you take up my e-mail space with your ignoble e-mails offering me magic pills that can help me enlarge a certain part of my body! Please, stop that! If you really want to help me, send me an elixir that can enlarge my whole body so I won't be interrogated by bewildered sales associates at JC Penney when I accidently enter the Big and Tall Department and try to find clothes for my not so big and tall physique.

Despite all the inattention I usually endure nearly every day, I eventually get some long overdue attention during political campaign seasons simply because I am an undecided voter. I have decided to remain undecided just to get the attention. I receive calls occasionally from the office of a political candidate giving me all sorts of tempting promises, such as subsidized healthcare, tax cuts, a balanced budget, clean renewable sources of energy, job security, etc. if I vote for their candidate. The next day I get more attractive offers from the office of another candidate. If you long to get some attention and respect as I do, all you need to do is become an undecided voter. You see, political candidates, as they say, are like the online lenders; when they compete, you win. The other day, I received a reassuring call from the Republican Party office promising me that if I vote Republican, they will invade a country of my choice! Can you meet or beat that Mr. Barack Obama!

We, the Short People

Christmas is the only time I feel really good about myself, thanks to the non-union workers in Santa's toy shop, the elves. They make me feel taller and handsomer! We, the short people, unapologetically resort to every possible excuse to promulgate our superiority. We claim that we are smarter, healthier, live longer, and not to mention, have a better sense of humor. But even if our claims are true, it is not because we are highly talented or are extraordinary human beings. It is because God is fair; God is righteous and he certainly knows how to compensate!

Once, drawing upon my wit, I told my female students that if they wanted to get married, they should make sure to find a short man. A short man makes an ideal husband. He is not only more economical to maintain, but a wife would also have the upper hand in the event she became involved in physical altercations with him. She could hit him on the head with her shoe very easily! Furthermore, the wife wouldn't suffer much emotionally if he leaves her! You see, the best way to avoid a costly lawsuit is to let others laugh at your expense!

For years we thought that socioeconomic status and opportunities were awarded by society based on established criteria such as, education, skills, productivity, experience, lineage, wealth, name recognition, etc. Therefore, a person's career success should normally be dependent on how many of these criteria a person can claim. Would you be surprised if you were told that your physical traits are also determining factors in how you are treated by society? We, the late immigrants especially, have always been reminded of the important role a good education plays in obtaining high-quality and high paying jobs. However, you may wonder how many other nonconventional factors may play a role for or against you when it comes to employment, livelihood, earning potential, and stereotyping. If you think that race, gender, age, religion, ethnicity, etc. are the only sources of bias, you may want to think again. In very subtle ways, our appearance, weight and especially height, have been proven to be other causes for discrimination.

We discriminate against ugly, overweight and yes, short people. Looking good is generously rewarded in the job market. Even though there are absolutely no grounds for an argument that ugly people are dumber or less efficient, it appears that good looking people get all the lucrative jobs. This leaves all the *do-you-want-fries-with-that* jobs for the not-so-good-looking people like me and you! The findings of some recent surveys may surprise you.

We learn from these findings that ugly women are paid 5 percent lower wages compared to the wage rate paid to average-looking women. Ugly men are punished even more severely. Their wage differential is even greater, a whopping 10 percent. I feel so sorry for you not-so-good-looking guys out there! Another researcher tells us that unattractive people earn 9 percent less and that after removing the effects of other factors such as education, experience, etc., beauty is rewarded by as much as 5 percent.

No doubt you would like to associate with the attractive folks. Beautiful people are not the only ones who reap the benefits of their beauty; their beauty also provides spillover pleasures for the rest of us. Quite simply in other words, society's overall level of pleasure is enhanced by having beautiful people around. This is similar to when some of my neighbors grow beautiful flower gardens in their yards every year, the whole neighborhood benefits from these gardens. As a matter of fact, I have been able to give flowers to my wife for every special occasion that arises during spring and summer, thanks to my neighbors. All I need to do is to wait until they leave their houses!

The physical discrimination situation is not any better for fat women; society punishes them for extra weight pound by pound. A woman who is 65 pounds overweight loses 7 percent of her earnings. That is more than 1 percent for every 10 pounds of weight. Luckily, the situation is much better for fat men because they are not noticeably punished for being overweight. What a welcome relief for those lazy coach potatoes! As a matter of fact, it is said that when it comes to marriage, some women want the man they live with to be fat because it makes them feel good about their own body. What a delusionary trick!

Even though, we can say so much more about the inverse correlation between economic success, obesity, and ugliness, the focus for this chapter is physical height and its impact on a person's economic success. You probably don't think that your height really matters when it comes to your monetary success. But does empirical evidence show that you earn more income if you are taller? While the positive correlation between height and earnings has been broadly observed, the rationale behind it was a mystery until recently.

I, of course, have known since I was a kid that height really matters. Anytime I went to a movie or attended a street performance, I missed about half of the show simply because I could hardly see over the head of the rest of the crowd almost all of whom were taller and bigger than me. Compulsory service in the Iranian army was also not much fun for me either. Even though I was the tallest in the last row which was reserved for the shortest trainees, I was the last person to get food, military respect, a chance to be sent home on weekends, and almost everything else.

Do you think most of the top corporate executives or elected government officials are tall by accident? With the exception of only five, it is said that all the presidents of the United States have been a few inches taller than average. Do you think that voters are likely to vote in favor of taller political candidates and discriminate against shorter? I bet they do. If you don't believe me, ask Michael Dukakis and Dennis Kucinich? Do you think tall people enjoy greater success because they simply receive preferential treatments during different stages of their lives? If your answer to all these questions is yes, you are unquestionably right.

Empirical evidence shows that taller people have more prestigious jobs and, therefore, earn higher salaries. According to a recent study, the average CEO is approximately 3 inches taller than the average American man who stands 5 feet 9 inches. Furthermore, 30 percent of CEOs are at least 6 feet 2 inches; the corresponding percentage for American adult men overall is only 3.9 percent. And according to other research conducted by two economic professors from Princeton University, four inches in height results in 10 percent additional earnings; that is 2.5 percent per every inch!

For years we hypothesized that tall people are more successful and paid more simply because they are treated favorably, especially during the early stages of their life. Why do you think taller people receive favorable treatment when it comes to employment? Is it because they are more qualified, more productive, better educated, better capable of handling dilemmatic situations, or intuitively better leaders? While all these speculations may have some merit, some researchers have been daring or imprudent enough to suggest that tall people are more successful simply because they are more intelligent! This was first asserted by the same two economists from Princeton University who both happen to be female and noticeably taller than average. While this assertion is heart breaking for those of us who might be vertically disadvantaged, it may not be as intuitive and straightforward as it sounds.

There are no scientific explanations or known genetic causes that demonstrate a direct tie between height and the level of intelligence; I hope! Some researchers argue that taller kids experience less mental deprivation at school, and are provided with more challenges and cognitive stimuli which help them to develop higher intellectual capability. Observations confirm that if you are tall while attending school, chances are that you will grow up to become a more successful adult later in life. That might be because teachers automatically pay more attention to taller students who are more dominant and more audacious in expressing themselves. Taller students are also more intensely involved in extracurricular programs and sport activities. Consequently, they gain leadership abilities, team playing skills and self confidence earlier in their lives; these skills and qualities will be sustained and even strengthened throughout their adult life.

Obviously, prettier and more handsome individuals are automatically considered more qualified for certain high paying jobs such as acting, modeling, hospitality, and more importantly, waiting tables at Hooters Restaurants. Consider all those so called

TV and movie stars; they are all taller than average with the exception of Danny DeVito. DeVito happens to be my favorite Hollywood star, not because he is a good actor, but because I usually save a bundle of money by purchasing most of my clothes from his annual garage sale! Taller people may receive premium pay, especially for the service related jobs requiring frequent contacts with clients, because employers believe that such individuals are more appealing to their customers and hence, they can improve the bottom lines of their businesses.

If you are discontented with your height as much as I am, do what I do. Use the metric system when you disclose your height to others. The other day I was calling around to find a proper dress suite to wear to a graduation ceremony. The lady who answered the phone asked me how tall I was and I told her that I was one thousand six hundred fifty millimeters! She said, "Wow, you must be enormously tall; I don't think we have any garments huge enough to fit you."

Cheer up and be grateful for whoever you are and how you look. "There is only one person in the whole world that looks exactly like you," as Mr. Fred Rogers used to say, "and that person is you."

Say No to Erectile Dysfunction

We are a nation of forward thinkers. Often we wish things would happen before their time. We sell the Sunday newspaper on Saturday. In the middle of the week, we wish our colleagues and coworkers a nice weekend. We sell next year's automobile models many months before the end of the current year, and often books that are released this year have a copyright date for next year. This growing phenomenon of anticipating things can be carried too far. Imagine if this "forward thinking" mentality was applied to the birth of a child. A child who is born today would have his birth date moved a few months ahead. Does that make him younger or is this just plainly weird? What if we sell wine before its time? Wouldn't that be promoting something of poor quality and bitter taste?

I am noticing that we may even be inventing solutions for imaginary problems, or problems that have not yet materialized. No, I am not talking about the preemptive strike and the WMD (weapons of mass destruction) fairytale that started our war with

Iraq. I am talking about *erectile dysfunction* or ED. Normally we seek a solution only if we encounter a problem. But looking ahead and creating a problem simply because we already have a solution on hand is indeed out of the ordinary. Sometimes I wonder if pharmaceutical companies have invented ED simply because they developed a drug for it. In other words, they have successfully created a dysfunction so that they could create a market for products like Viagra and other male potency brands. Advertizing is designed to manipulate potential consumers by leading them to believe that they have a problem that needs fixing even though they didn't have the problem before they viewed a particularly persuasive commercial.

I question whether ED as a condition even exists. In my experience, the male sex organ is a remarkably self-regulating appendage that for the most part works perfectly. As a matter of fact, it seems like it is the only part of a man's body that has a "mind of its own." Its self-regulating, self-propelling mechanism kicks in and drives it to function without your permission even while you are asleep. How many times, when you woke up early in the morning, did you have to rush to the public bath house before sunrise to perform the mandatory religious duty of *Ghosle Jenabat?* (It is an Islamic mandate that a man must wash his body in a certain way after ejaculating whether it happens while he is asleep or while he is awake) Do you think that the public bathhouses back home in Iran would have accumulated such large profits if male organs were not functioning perfectly?

After reflection, I would say that erectile dysfunction is not as big of a problem as advertisers want us to believe. Perhaps they are playing on men's insecurities and fear of inadequacy. If there is an erection, it means the male organ is functioning. The only time there is a dysfunction is when there is no erection. Even if there is dysfunction, we don't need laboratory-made chemical compounds to treat it. Relax, don't worry if you are unable to find or cannot afford pharmacological solutions; you can always find cheaper substitutes. Who said the remedy for ED has to be expensive or come in a bottle? How about the inexpensive purchase of *Sport Illustrated Magazine's* swim suit edition, or in my case a free copy of *Victoria's Secret* catalogue? What about leisurely things such as stress-reliving activities?

As a matter of fact, we Iranians have already invented a high potency workable solution for ED using high calorie natural food ingredients, and we did this long before the discovery of Viagra. We use a blend of sesame seed oil and date syrup called *Ardeh Shireh*. It has helped millions of men to regain the experience of intimacy that they had lost in their lives. This combination of natural food ingredients is not only stimulating, but also delicious and much cheaper than Viagra. The added bonus of this natural alternative is that you don't need a doctor visit or a prescription to buy it.

Even if a man is unable to have an erection, why should this be considered a problem? This situation could be considered a blessing if you take into account the enormous amount of money and aggravation that could be saved as a result. Romance is expensive both for the individuals involved and for society. Do you know how much money is squandered as a result of a man's erection? Although there are no reliable statistics, according to CNN estimates, a whopping $138 per man is spent on Valentine's Day alone. If one takes the long view beyond Valentine's Day, the financial ramifications of having an erection are even more ominous. This is often the pattern: a man sees an attractive woman; he pays to romance the woman; he falls in love; he gets married and pays for a wedding and honeymoon; he has kids and pays for all of their needs as they grow up; he buys a house; and he not only has to make a mortgage payment every month, but he has to go to Home Depot everyday to buy more expensive stuff! Using the words of a famous Persian song, romance is not cheap. *Atr khahad, chatr khahad, poodr khahad, kif khahad, kafsh khahad yare khoshgel,* or "The beautiful ladies want perfume, a purse, powders, and an umbrella" (rough translation).

In addition to all the aforementioned personal financial consequences, consider how much money we as a society spend on prosecuting sexual offenders, keeping them behind bars, or keeping them under surveillance. How much money could we save as tax payers if we didn't have to pay for the promiscuity and sexual indiscretion of our politicians? Remember Eliot Spitzer and his $1,000 an hour call girls. Consider the billions of dollars that are wasted by pharmaceutical companies on advertising male potency drugs, despite the fact that we cannot buy them directly. Have you seen some of their TV commercials lately? My favorite is the one that shows a young couple engaging in what looks like sexual stimulation. Slowly they start to unbutton each other's shirts and suddenly there is a voice saying, "When the moment is right, will you be ready?" After a few seconds, the ad shows the same couple in the middle of a huge corn field. Why would you go to the middle of a corn field when the moment is right? We have heard stories of people doing it in the backseat of their car, on first-class seats of an airplane, in a phone booth, in parents' bed rooms, in public bathrooms especially in the Minneapolis Airport! and even in St. Patrick's Cathedral in New York City! All of these places are bad enough, but it boggles my mind to think that people might want to do it in the middle of a dusty, uncomfortable corn field under the watchful eyes of hundreds of scarecrows; come on! And I ask myself, what would you do if the moment is right and she is not ready? Isn't that like spending a good sum of money and a great deal of time on preparing a delicious gourmet meal, but when it is time to sit down and eat the woman has no appetite.

When Viagra first came along, the advertizing agencies had difficulty finding people who were willing to appear in their promotional TV commercials. There was a stigma attached to being labeled as impotent, and even worse, to be seen by millions of viewers in a male potency drug commercial. However, this is no longer the case; this initial reluctance has all but disappeared. Now, even young couples very willingly and happily acknowledge their sexual impotency. In all of my life I have never seen so many happy couples smiling over the matter of sexual dysfunction. If ED is a problem in a couple's relationship, why would they be so happy and why would they even brag about it? Shouldn't they be a little embarrassed and bit more discreet about it? I believe the reality is that those who appear in such testimonial ads are not ordinary people suffering with ED. They are actors and actresses who are happy because they know that they are perfectly functioning sexual beings.

Once I was contacted by one of those so-called marketing research companies. A representative from the company told me that she was conducting a survey in my area, and was soliciting consumer opinions regarding the effectiveness of the Viagra advertising campaign. I was one of those chosen at random to take the survey. She asked me if I had any ideas about how the Viagra advertising campaign could be more successful. I said that I did. I told her that I think that the efficacy of the advertising would increase if the advertisers used a *before* and *after* format to visually show the viewers what happens after they use Viagra. She told me that was an interesting idea and asked me if I had any suggestions on how it could be implemented. I told her I did have a suggestion. Being the economist that I am, I think of every thing in the context of demand and supply. I suggested that they could use a demand curve, a down-sloping line, to illustrate one's *before* condition, and a supply curve, an up-sloping line, to illustrate one's *after* condition.

Some greedy entrepreneurs have gone even further. They cynically try to sell naive consumers male enhancement drugs and other products that can help them enlarge certain part of their body. Come on, you must think that we are utterly stupid. If we bought such an elixir, males would no longer brag with all-knowing bravado about their favorite sport teams, nor would they brag about all of the fantastic deals they negotiate every day. All they would talk about and brag about would be their magnificent body parts, their manhood and what "chick magnets" they have become! This reminds me of a news story I read recently about an incident that occurred at a busy airport. A man was arrested by customs agents and accused of smuggling into the United States three exotic snakes which the agents believed were hidden in the man's pants. However, after a close body examination, they discovered that there were really only two snakes in his pants! Do you think this man overdosed on male enhancement drugs or used them after their expiration date had already passed?

And please, if pharmaceutical companies are going to make such miraculous drugs, the least they could do is make them available to us without a prescription. They could do us a favor if they cut out the middlemen. Why should I have to go to my doctor and beg him, in front of his nurse and possibly his office personnel, to prescribe for me Viagra or other male enhancement drugs? I have already had an experience of being embarrassed because I was so naïve. As an economics educator, I get a lot of mail related to my professional activity. I responded once to an invitation promising me a free dinner just for attending a free workshop on ED. What do you think ED means to an economist like me? Of course I thought it was a free workshop on the economic topic of *Elasticity of Demand*. Imagine how embarrassed I was when I got there and discovered that the workshop wasn't about elasticity of demand; it was about *Erectile Dysfunction*.

Finally, I want to make a plea to the pharmaceutical companies to make the male enhancement drugs generally physically enhancing, and not be so specific. I don't need to enlarge only certain parts of my body. I could really benefit from something that could help me enlarge the whole me so that the next time I need to buy cloths for myself, I won't have to wait for Mr. Danny DeVito to have a garage sale!. And if the pharmaceutical companies insist on keeping their enhancement drugs so specific, I wish they would make something that enlarges people's brains. Now, that is something we really need in this country. I wonder if it would be a big seller.

Part III

Ruminations

Culprit by Default

Working in a restaurant when I was a student in the early 1970s wasn't officially authorized under my student visa, but it provided me with a badly needed income. Earning a salary by the hour was something unheard of for me since there was no payment system like that back home in Iran. Even though the minimum wage rate in those days was not all that high in nominal terms, it was a considerable amount of money for me since I used to live on a very small stipend. In addition to its monetary reward, the job had non-monetary benefits. I was able to take home the restaurant's unsold leftover baked potatoes every night because I believe that health department regulations did not allow the potatoes to be saved. I would take them back to my dormitory where a roommate and a couple of hungry friends awaited me. Some nights, if I was really lucky, I would return to the dormitory with a half a dozen baked potatoes; when this happened, we would all enjoy a big feast.

People who lived in the small town in the U.S. where I was going to college were not shy about disclosing their feelings of mistrust toward me because I was an immigrant. Initially, given the sporadic abnormal behavior of some of the foreign students at my school, I thought that harboring feelings of mistrust was not that much out of the ordinary. However, over time I came to see that this was not acceptable. Every night after closing time, we workers had to stay in the restaurant for a couple of hours to perform the unpleasant jobs of cleaning up and taking out the garbage. One night, as we were cleaning the restaurant and getting ready for closing, there was suddenly a power outage. It became very dark everywhere. The darkness didn't bother me at all. In fact the darkness kind of made me feel at home because when I was growing up we didn't have much electricity, and we had to maneuver in the dark or in dim light quite a bit. But the manager, who was also the owner of the restaurant, was caught by surprise. Apparently because he couldn't see me in the dim light of his flashlight, he was repeatedly inquiring about me by asking in a loud, probing voice, "Where is Reza? Where is Reza?" For a brief second I thought to myself that it was very nice that he was concerned about my well-being. It didn't take long for me to come to my senses. I could tell from the tone of his voice and my quick recollection of his past treatment of me that he was not looking for me out of a sense of altruism. He was looking for me because he was perhaps thinking that I might take advantage of the chaotic situation, and run away with his money or something else from his restaurant. It was a very disheartening experience to be judged in this way when I had never given the owner cause to mistrust me.

That was not, of course, the only incident of this kind that I experienced. One time I went to a garage sale. It was the first time I had gone to a garage sale, and it was such an exhilarating experience for me because we didn't have anything like that back home in Iran. Everything was on display so I knew the garage sale was going on but I could see nobody on the premises. After a quick look around, I left the garage and was walking toward my car—a Ford Maverick—not to be mistaken for the maverick we didn't send to White House! I hurriedly went toward my car so that I could move on to the next garage sale. All of a sudden as I was turning the key in the ignition to start the car, a lady came out of the house walking toward my car as fast as her feet would carry her. She inspected the inside of my car visually but thoroughly; she wanted to make sure that I didn't steal any of the junk she was trying to get rid of from her garage. When I think about incidents such as these, incidents in which I have been judged and presumed outright guilty when I did nothing to warrant such treatment, it still hurts my feelings. This kind of prejudicial treatment is unjust and degrading when directed toward a person who holds cherished values of honesty and decency. I had no choice but to endure these insults then; I saw them as the by-product of my moving from a third world country to an affluent nation. However, rationalizing discrimination in this way made it no less painful to endure.

I still continue to be the target of hasty judgment, imaginary offense, and discriminatory accusation even after all the years I have lived in this country; however, as time has passed these incidents may have become just a little more subtle. I try not to take these offensive reactions to my foreignness seriously; I often shrug them off with a humorous comment. What else can I do? When the going is tough, humor is a must! I remember an incident that took place in the health club I usually go to a few days a week; it happened in the sauna which is my favorite room in this entire huge club. It is the steam heated room you share with many other people who are all semi-naked. The presence of female club members seems to give the men an enticement to brag about something just to get the attention of the women. Because these men are unclothed, one can readily see that they don't have much to brag about in terms of their physical attributes. Therefore, they boast about other things that anybody can brag about without fear of ridicule. They brag about the great deal they shrewdly negotiated on a new car, or how successfully they squared off with their insurance company, but most often they brag about their favorite sport and sports team. I believe some people are natural born show offs who have to brag about everything. I hate it, especially when they brag about baseball which they always seem to do. They could care less if a catastrophic disaster leveled the entire town just as long as the baseball fields remained intact. After living in this country for more than three and a half decades, I still don't know anything about baseball, much to the chagrin of my children. Often I had to bear the humiliation of watching baseball games with them like a dummy. Without a doubt I knew they would eventually ask me a question to test my knowledge of baseball, and sure enough they did. They wanted to know who my favorite baseball player was, as if I knew the names of all the players. I wanted to be seen as someone who was in the loop so I told them Shaquille O'Neal was my favorite baseball player; I had heard that famous athlete's name somewhere and crossed my fingers. Of course, I had to endure my embarrassment when I could tell from my children's sly laughter that I had made a wrong guess.

Now back to the key point of my health club experience of discrimination. I was in the sauna with a bunch of such overweening guys when suddenly someone entered the room, looked at me kind of angrily and asked, "Are you done with that?" The object he was referring to was a piece of weightlifting equipment that someone had brought into the sauna before I had entered; of course, it didn't belong in the sauna room. I really had no clue about what led him to believe that I was the guilty party; I could only guess that he accused me simply because I was the only one in the room who didn't look quite like the others. This kind of mentality, that you are presumed guilty if you don't look like everyone else, has become even more intense after the disastrous events of 9/11. The day after terrorists crashed planes into the World Trade Center, the Pentagon, and a field in Pennsylvania, a colleague of mine asked me sarcastically "What are you going to do now?" The person seemed to be implying that now that I had successfully completed the attacks of the day before, I was now in the process of mapping my next destructive strategy. It was perhaps his chronic distrust and bigoted attitude toward me as a member of a "lesser culture" that were being manifested in that question. It still surprises me when I encounter such judgmental attitudes and the ignorance beneath them in so-called intelligent people. It also continues to surprise me when these attitudes are expressed by people who have lived their whole lives in a country which proudly identifies itself as a "melting pot" of diverse people, avows that "all men are created equal," and espouses that a person is supposed to be judged by the "the content of their character" alone. I thought, and still think that individuals like my colleague are creatures of a lop-sided mass media that consistently and convincingly promotes wrong attitudes and unfounded ideas which are based in ignorance and cultural elitism.

I believe this kind of elitist mentality has led to the attitude in this country that "we are the best and the heck with all the rest." Fixation on such a self-indulgent mentality and limited world perspective means that we are not open to the possibility that others may also have good ideas. I wholeheartedly think that we as a nation have suffered enough collectively from this kind of mentality, especially economically in this age of global interconnectedness. It particularly has made us ignorant of the gradual rise to power of other countries and has blinded us to the idea that others matter. Many of us are not eager to open ourselves to the ideas expressed by others; unless "the other" is just like us, we have no desire to accept him or her with open hearts and open minds. For example, it took an "energy crisis" to force auto makers in this country to finally realize that the best fuel-efficient cars are not made in the U.S., and the consumer's love affair with inefficient, gas-guzzling American cars and trucks would soon be coming to an end because of soaring gas prices. This arrogance, greed, "isolationism," and lack of foresight has led to the economic failure of the once invincible American car industry, not to mention the resulting increase in the government deficit because of financial bailouts/loans to these companies, and the loss of jobs for American workers.

Maybe the best way to describe such an attitude is to invoke the famous phrase "American exceptionalism" that has been used eccentrically by neoconservatives to theorize that the U.S. has a particular doctrinal superiority over other advanced nations when it comes to social, political, and economic systems. Such a generalized fixation on ourselves and our attitude of superiority precludes us from learning from the experiences of other nations, many of which are more successful than the U.S. particularly with respect to important areas such as education, healthcare, and social justice. Only sheer arrogance and a misguided understanding of what it means to be a world "leader" could explain why we as a country would not want to learn from the successes and failures of other nations in order to advance our national goals. Success in a global economy requires that we think outside of the box of fascination with ourselves. We can learn a lot even from a "dummy" as a current popular TV ad would suggest. Ideas from others may not create Nirvana, but they have the potential, if we open our minds, to stimulate creative problem-solving, and pave the way for alternative views of how we can accomplish many important goals in a variety of areas. In order for this to happen we must be willing and able to let go of our notions of superiority, and re-identify ourselves as one positively contributing nation among many in a global world community.

I will end with a story that is partially fictional, but is intended to humorously invite you into the world of a Muslim immigrant in this country. I particularly like the story for its entertainment value which takes the edge off of painful feelings of being discriminated against. I used to live in a community where my close neighbors not only thought I was a dummy, but they also held suspicions that I was a member of a sleeper terrorist cell. One day, when I was leisurely enjoying barbequing in my backyard, much to my surprise I found myself confronted by a couple of local police officers. They proceeded to inform me that my neighbors reported to them that they suspected I was enriching uranium in my backyard and that I might be trying to construct nuclear bombs! They perhaps reported to the police that I came from Iran and, of course, that's what Iranians are suspected of doing these days. After I somewhat recovered from my stunned incredulity, it took me some time to verbally explain that I was not a terrorist, and to demonstrate to the police officers that I was in fact making shish kabobs. Granted I created a little smoke, but barbeque smoke never killed any one as far as I knew. Also, I had to plead with them not to confiscate my newly purchased Weber gas grill because they thought it was a mobile nuclear lab! This story may seem a little far-fetched but it exemplifies the rush to judgment and the preconceived bigoted notions that people who fear diversity inflict on others who are different in native origin, skin color, culture, and religion. Just as the U.S. as a country must economically and politically change its view of itself to reflect that it is a member of a community of nations, so too must individual U.S. citizens change their exclusionary views of other U.S. citizens who reflect that very same community of nations.

Overcrowding,
No Excuse for Complaint

I just returned to the United Stats from a short but exciting trip to Iran. While visiting the major cities of Iran, one thing that grabs your attention more than anything else is *overcrowding* which is best manifested in their chaotic traffic conditions and the proliferation of residential high-rises. Almost everyone is furious about this because they see overcrowding as a social evil and they complain about how this increased presence of others has made his or her life more uncomfortable or down right difficult. There are some people who think that certain other people do not deserve to live in big cities like Tehran. In other words, they don't hesitate to express their lack of tolerance for others especially for Tehran's poorer, less fortunate citizens. People in these big cities also tell odd stories about traffic accidents almost all of which are caused by other careless drivers and not themselves. They tell you how lucky they feel when they return home after work without being involved in an accident. You can see the most visible signs of overcrowding in the streets of Tehran, a city of more than 10 million inhabitants. A colossal number of automobiles are speeding swiftly alongside many motorcycles, and pedestrians are walking in different directions as confidently and fearlessly as if they are walking in their own private driveway. Many of these cars are very old and are in substandard mechanical condition. Most of them are moving air-polluting machines and they are extremely noisy because they are not properly maintained. The chaotic traffic made me quite jittery when I was getting a joy ride from a friend in his brand new Toyota Camry. I asked him if he was afraid of getting involved in an accident with his new car. He told me that the cost of repairing cars after accidents and having to pay traffic tickets are the implicit costs of driving your car on the streets of Tehran. He added with amusement that a portion of his monthly earnings is devoted to such routine precautionary expenses.

In defiance of the conventional wisdom, I want to challenge the notion that overcrowding is an annoyance by stating that I instead see overcrowding as a blessing. No one coerces you to live in a crowded city; you do so voluntarily. You obviously enjoy the life amenities that are only available in big cities: restaurants, theatres, cultural events, fancy stores, shopping malls, recreational conveniences, and I would add to this list, crowds. You benefit from these amenities even though they may come with some inconveniences and, of course, higher costs of living. One reason people often choose to live in crowded cities is because they expect to earn more income. Those of you who constantly complain about overcrowding need to remember that the main sources of your higher income are the other people who you feel are annoyingly taking up your space. How are you going to earn your income if the other people around you do not spend money paying for your goods or services? Whether we like it or not, we are very economically interdependent people.

Another way to view the benefits of overcrowding is to also remember that we produce wealth and boost our income by utilizing productivity-enhancing technology, and that technology is created by other talented individuals. All life-enhancing ideas, the building blocks of economic progress, originate from individuals. People are the source of capital, information, and technology, the necessary ingredients of wealth and income. Accordingly, the larger the number of people who live with you in a crowed big city, the better your prospects for enjoying the benefits that come with high level technological advances, international commerce, state-of-the-art healthcare services, good schools, and hopefully a great career with a high salary. Only people can exploit ways to transform new ideas into useful products, wealth, and income generating schemes, and crowed big cities are the hubs where all of this happens.

Historically, human life started to improve as soon as we learned how to urbanize and live together. Since that time human communities have became richer and wealthier; we discovered ways in which we could make more and better products that enhanced our living and enabled us to work fewer numbers of hours to accomplish things. Gradually, progressive technology enabled us to imagine, invent, and produce high-tech products such a refrigerators that can send your grocery store an electronic signal when you are about to run out of milk or meat. Almost our entire economic growth happened within the last two hundred years, particularly after the Industrial Revolution in the early 19th century. One of the consequences of the Industrial Revolution was the mobilization of the labor force and the massive movement of workers into industrial jobs, thus augmenting the productivity of labor. We learned how to improve our life as soon as we learned how to live together. Economic progress requires wealth, and wealth is the fruit of knowledge and technology that are created by human beings. Furthermore, entrepreneurial activities are driven by profit which in turn boosts mass production and mass consumption. Big companies could not have survived if it were not for the millions and millions of people willing and able to buy their products.

When I say that people should not complain about overcrowding, this should not be construed as an unconditional claim that overcrowding does not create any problems. Overcrowding is a problem, but not for those who make a conscious decision to live in an overcrowded city instead of in a small town. Many people cannot flourish unless they live in big cities. Modern products and innovative services cannot be developed in rural areas. Likewise, overcrowding is not a problem for those of us whose welfare is not adversely affected as a result of it. There are, however, people who always complain because they either cannot afford the expenses of living in a big city or they are unwilling to tolerate other people. Overcrowding should not be a daunting challenge for a municipal government that has the means and the power to provide adequate infrastructure to accommodate a sprawling population. However, municipal government may often fail to meet this challenge. The advantages that come along with living in a city with a large population can be realized and augmented only through proper governmental policies. Lack of, or improper municipal government policies can simply ruin the advantages of big city living. This can happen if government creates an atmosphere of uncertainty regarding the delivery of needed city services such as those related to safety and health, neglects the repair and replacement of basic infrastructures, and doesn't effectively manage traffic by eliminating or minimizing traffic bottlenecks. Thus, the big city benefits derived from human creativity and voluntary entrepreneurial trade will suffer and eventually may simply be eliminated. Should this happen, what are left are only the tensions, hassles, discontents, and vulgarities of an angry, unhappy, big population of people. If overcrowding per se was a hindrance to economic progress, highly populous countries like China should be the most backward nation in the world, and as we know it is not. To the contrary, it is the most economically flourishing country in the world with the highest annual growth rate of any nation.

There are additional conditions that must be met given that population in and of itself is not the source of wealth. Population can be a source of wealth, if the rights of individuals, especially property rights, are duly protected by government and respected by all. There are indeed many highly populated countries in which living conditions are deplorable; this is a factual testament that population per se is not a sufficient condition for economic growth. Institutional settings should also be favorable to and supportive of individuals' basic rights, the ethical enforcement of contracts, the utilization of practices that promote the safe and efficient execution of business transactions, and above all, ensuring that the rule of law is followed. These are critical building blocks of economic prosperity. In the absence of these institutional factors with their accompanying controls and oversight, a country cannot move forward no matter how intelligent, creative, and entrepreneurial its population may be. In other words, the advantages of a large population will not materialize automatically if institutional practices are not conducive to ensuring posterity. A big city population without effective and supportive institutional factors could be compared to having millions of modern automobiles but no modern highway system to accommodate them and move them forward. Calamity will ensue in the wake of such a lack of foresight and mismanagement.

I believe that the advantages of living in a big city are not limited to pecuniary gains either. We enjoy the opportunity to socialize and chat with our neighbors. We learn through interaction with others. We borrow things from one another and also do business with each other. We help one another when a need arises. We quite simply obtain personal satisfaction and our lives are enriched when we associate with others. Of course, these are ideal and welcomed occasions for human interaction. We know there are also times when you wish that a particular person was not living in your neighborhood such as when the person is a social nuisance, a thief, con-artist, a child molester, or someone who tries to rip you off by never returning the tools you lend to them. It is a rare happening when a neighborhood doesn't have someone who is just plain disagreeable and is always shouting "Get off my lawn." These are usually situations when human interaction is something to be avoided and not embraced.

Even though people grumble and complain about living in a crowded city, deep down they usually don't mean it. That is why they live in such cities to begin with. We live in a crowded city because we like the enormous advantageous opportunities that can only be found in big cities. Aren't these advantages created because there are so many people working for a better life for themselves and others?

I offer an additional perspective on the benefits of overcrowding. Society might benefit from a family's decision to have more children because the spillover benefits are enjoyed by society while the costs of raising children remain with the family. If my courageous friend has seven kids, you as a neighbor may benefit from his sacrifice. You gain at his expense. His kids do not make resources any less available to you. On the contrary, his children spend their money and help your business. They drive the wage rate down. They baby sit your children. They often do work that many of us don't want to do such as raking our leaves, shoveling our snow, or cutting our grass. Whether they are the result of choice or chance, good children are good for society. They contribute to new ideas by bringing a young, fresh perspective to old problems. If raised with good values and a sense of community service, most of them become productive citizens, future leaders, and movers and shakers. They contribute to creative ideas and diversity of perspective at no cost to society. All the costs of having children stay with my friend who is responsible for raising them. The personal resources available to my friend's family will, of course, have to be divided among a larger number of kids so this diminishes the share each child will receive. However, the overall level of resources available to you as a citizen will not diminish. In summary, the benefits of having more kids are externalized while the costs are internalized. It is, therefore, erroneous to assume that everyone is worse off because my friend has more children. He may be the one who is worse off, but society as a whole is not. By having a large number of children, his consumption of economic resources does not have any adverse impact on his neighbors and fellow citizens. As long as he can afford to raise his children to become productive members of society when they grow up, his children will not make society any less fortunate or prosperous. However, if they do not make positive contributions to society as adults, this may force the government to support them at everybody's expense through the provision of welfare services, training or rehab programs, and in worse case scenarios, paying for more police officers and expanded correctional institutions and programs. All these things may use up limited governmental resources that might otherwise have been used for more positive and productive alternative purposes.

Again, I would like to emphasize that having more children does not automatically benefit society. Having more children benefits society as long as the children do not grow up to become criminals and/or freeloaders. Generally speaking, I might add, more children may make society worse off because parents need to spend more time taking care of their kids and less time on other matters that can help elevate their standard of living. Society does benefit, though, with one caveat: the family must be able to provide for all of its children adequately. If not, all of the costs of raising kids may not stay with the family because, as in United States, the burden of welfare payments and programs falls on the shoulders of taxpayers. Having more children without being able to support them is obviously not going to benefit anybody.

Moving from the economic level to the interpersonal level, the fallacious judgment some would venture to make is that if I were not born, everyone else would be better off. It is interesting to ponder what kind of impact one's life has had on society not just on an economic level but on a relational level as well. It is a mental exercise using one's imagination similar to what actor James Stewart went through in the movie *It's a Wonderful Life.* Imagine what life would be like if your influence as a person was erased from places, situations and the lives of others. The movie made it poignantly clear that human beings impact societal conditions and the lives of other human beings in ways that are not always immediately and concretely known to them. On the surface I guess I could say that if I was not born only the rest of my family might have been financially better off, not anyone else. Everyone else would be the same. But if you follow the simple yet profound thread of the movie one can see that the existence of every human being impacts a whole host of people and situations. This is true whether you are like the economically poor but generous and caring George Bailey, or the economically rich but greedy and ruthless Henry Potter. When I stop a moment and quickly ponder the impact my life has made as a son, husband, father, and educator on the lives of my parents, wife, children, and students, to name just a few, I find that I don't need the angel Clarence to help me see that it is indeed a wonderful life. Also, consider the following image when thinking about the benefits of overcrowding and interpersonal interaction. Life is like a cell phone, you enjoy it a lot more if other people have it and use it. The more other people use their cell phones, the more you enjoy yours. If the only thing I can do is to say "hi" and brighten your day by smiling at you, as far as I'm concerned, that is one little thing among so many more niceties that makes life worth living.

And finally, the last time I was in Iran I was given an opportunity to talk to high school students in my hometown. I found most of them bright, articulate, enthusiastic, and eager to learn. They answered my questions with a high level of sophistication that revealed their maturity. I had no doubt that many of them, who came from a crowded family, will grow up to be future leaders, movers and shakers, who will utilize their power to improve the life of others in Iran or elsewhere in the world. You see, having and raising children can be likened to archaeological excavations. Archeologists spend months or even years digging the ground expecting to find something of great historical value. They may not find something every time they dig in the ground. However, when they find even one significant item, that one item reveals a great deal of valuable information about us as a society and our history. Similarly with our children, they can be society's great treasures and the repositories of our society's history and values.

Being Afraid of Your Own Death

The premature death of one of my former students was an occasion that caused me to become reflective about my own eventual mortality. Death is the most inexplicable, the most undesirable, and the most certain event in everybody's life. Well, maybe death is not the only certainty in life if one considers the well-used adage of Benjamin Franklin: "In this world nothing can be said to be certain except death and taxes." It has also been frequently said that we can't cheat death or avoid taxes; however, we sure try every machination we can think of to do both. Just as we utilize every conceivable scheme, legal and sometimes not so legal, to minimize our tax payments, we also resort to a variety of measures, including unconventional ones, to try to postpone our physical demise.

In the United States and other high income countries, our efforts to try to cheat death and conceal the physical evidence of our aging have become big business. We follow strict diet programs, and try to eat our daily minimum requirement of fruits and vegetables as recommended by health experts. We exercise on a regular basis and do our part to put money into the coffers of gyms, health clubs, and personal trainers. We take our daily vitamins and food supplements, often out of a bottle, (thank God we have the technology to do that) just to be on the safe side in case we may not have "hit the mark" with our healthy diet regimen. We avoid engaging in risky activities that could put our life and limbs in jeopardy, and we almost religiously try not to miss our preventive medical and dental check-ups.

When we get older, we do foolish things to pretend to ourselves and others that we are still young, attractive, energetic and virile. We dye our graying and thinning hair, or purchase wigs and toupees if we don't have enough hair to dye. We dress in colorful clothes hoping these will distract from the pallor of our aging skin, and we choose youthful styles that at times reveal parts of our bodies that most people would rather not see. We replace our missing teeth with prosthetic devices, or spend a fortune on teeth whitening procedures. We try to reconstruct the badly depreciated components of our body parts through plastic surgery, implants, and copious injections of Botox. We drive racy sports cars often in bright eye-catching colors with convertible tops, and rejoice in getting rid of the family SUV with its baby seats. In short, we do everything at our disposal to either hide or postpone the degrading implications and manifestations of old age which remind us of the inevitability of approaching death. We may successfully simulate a more youthful appearance and fool ourselves for a few additional years, but all of our efforts certainly fail to return youthful vitality to our bodies and sharp mental acuity to our minds and memory.

We might be fascinated by the death of others, but we are certainly not fascinated by our own. Understandably, no one relishes contemplating one's own demise. We find it very difficult to dwell on the fact that one day, and who knows what day, all that we have come to know and love, all that we have given our life to, will go on without us. We will just be a memory in the minds of others, and at that, only for a while. We don't want to face death, or talk about it, or even to think about it. We try to ignore it as if it will never happen at all, especially when we are young. When we were young, death was not on our mind. It was all about life unless tragically one of our young friends died for whatever reason; perhaps then we may have paused for a moment to think about death. But we didn't stay with the thought for very long. We had too many things to do and many people to meet; and besides, we thought to ourselves that it won't happen to me. We thought of our life as a straight line with no end in sight.

This effort to avoid the inevitable is not, of course, something new. We human beings have always tried very diligently to discover new sources of longevity, to search for the "fountain of youth," and to unlock the mystery of everlasting life. In the United States and other high income countries, people hate aging and the resulting physical deterioration. We spend several billion dollars every year on genetic research and expensive experiments hoping to prolong our life span for even a few more years. Such efforts have been, to some extent, successful. Today in many countries the average life expectancy has improved considerably. In highly developed countries like the United States, the average life expectancy is approaching or exceeding 80 years. This life expectancy is almost twice as much as what it was for people who lived in the Middle Ages. It is worth mentioning that a great deal of this progress has happened during the last few decades. An April, 2008 brief issued by the Congressional Budget Office (CBO) contained a couple of interesting statistics that give a sense of the general progress we have made in terms of increasing life expectancy. The life expectancy for men born in 2004 was 75.2 years, almost 10 years longer than men born in 1950. The life expectancy for women born in 2004 was 80.4 years, more than 9 years greater than for women born in 1950.

The rising average life expectancy, however, has not changed the way we think about death. Our fear and active resistance to death have not diminished. In other words, longer life has not made death any less sufferable for us because the tragic end of our life is dreadful no matter what our age. The sobering truth is that we know not the day or the hour. Death is just as close to us at the age of 10, 20 or 30 as it is at the age of 80 or 90. Even though the thought of death is unbearable for most people, we have all heard of cases of extreme physical suffering where loved ones or the suffering person pray for the blessed relief that death will bring. We have also heard of cases where a person experiencing intense depression, hopelessness, and emotional isolation choose to take their own life, again, in search of the relief and peace of death. However, most human beings want to savor life as long as possible and find that choosing to die is almost unimaginable.

In some sense, a life of 80 years seems as short as the life of 30 or 40 years. In my experience and the experience of others I have talked with, our perception of time begins to change after a certain age. I remember when I was a kid, one hour of waiting felt like a whole day. Now, at almost 60 years of age, one-week of waiting feels like a day. It seems that time passes more quickly as we get older. We may find ourselves asking more and more often, "Where has the time gone?" The seasons of the year seem to come and go more quickly. Birthdays, our own and those of others, seem to come upon us more rapidly. The years feel like they are piling up very quickly and soon we find ourselves applying for Medicare and getting AARP (American Association of Retired Persons) membership material in the mail. It seems like just yesterday your child was born, and in no time at all he/she is graduating from college, getting married and having his or her own children. Suddenly you find yourself with a new identity and a new role in life, that of grandparent. We look at our grandchildren and pray to God that we will be able to walk with them as far and as long as possible along the journey of their lives. Welcoming a new life and watching your family grow and expand can intensify our fear of death. We want to tighten our grip on life; we want to be there for it all, but this makes it even harder to face the inevitable reality of letting go.

I don't believe that there is a reasonable correlation between the length of our life and the quality of our living. In other words, a happy life does not depend on how long we live. It really comes down to the cliché, the simple but profound cliché, "Life (whether long or short) is what you make it." Age is not a distinguishing factor when it comes to being a miserable human being; you can choose to be miserable no matter what your age. No one and no thing can make a person miserable; we make ourselves miserable by how we view the life that has been given to us. The persons and events of our lives can be seen as either a blessing or a curse. Whichever one we decide upon will shape who and how we are as a human being, and our life will become a blessing or a curse for others. According to the available evidence, people in the Middle Ages, who lived much shorter lives than we do, definitely were less fearful of death than we are today. I believe with some degree of confidence, that a good many people in the Middle Ages lived a happier and a less stressful life mainly because they were more spiritual in those days. I think they were more moderate in life style and materialistic expectations; they seemed closer to nature and to God, and maintained stronger moral values.

To those who believe in God and in judgment day, death is only a transition from this world to a better one. According to a report in the Wall Street Journal, nearly 70 percent of people who live in the United States suffer from some kind of psychological disorder caused by fear, anxiety, and stress. The report also noted that fear, anxiety, and stress were the result of excessive absorption with material life. (Those of us who are not absorbed in material life will have to wait until our psychological problems are eventually discovered!) Death is frightening to those who are devoted to hedonistic culture, the main purpose of which is the accumulation of wealth and power. Material possessions and power will not keep one from death and become meaningless to a dead man.

Can we learn anything from giving thoughtful consideration to our own death? I believe we can. Such consideration, at the very least, generates some serious questions that need more attention. Should we change our conduct in light of the fact that we have no control over our own inevitable demise? Should we modify our greed-dominated life because in the end, possessions and power mean nothing? Should we pursue a quality of life marked by love and compassion toward other people? Should we re-examine our goals and priorities and make more meaningful adjustments before it is too late? Should we ask ourselves what is the best use of the precious time that we have been given in this too short life? I believe we should answer "yes" to all of the above.

Raising Bicultural Children

S ometimes when I speak over the phone with the parents of some of my bicultural students, I hear parents at the other end of the line speaking with heavy accents. It is not long before I come to realize that these parents are experiencing and struggling with the same problems I encounter as a parent who is trying to raise bicultural kids. Child rearing is never easy for any parent, but raising bicultural children brings an additional unique set of problems and is quite a formidable challenge. Often this requires an extra measure of patience and an extra measure of wisdom. As immigrant parents, we strive on a daily basis to determine what is acceptable and what is unacceptable for our children. We constantly search for the best way to reconcile the differences between our native culture and the dominant culture in America, and find feasible methods of assimilation or acculturation. Almost daily we as parents are called upon to make decisions and do things that will hopefully guide our children through the acculturation process by encouraging them to learn about and value their own cultural heritage, and to not give in to the lure of total assimilation.

Acculturation and assimilation can be viewed as two opposite ends of a spectrum. Acculturation is the process whereby the attitudes and/or behaviors of people from one culture are somewhat modified as a result of contact with another culture. Acculturation implies attitudes of mutual respect which enable some elements of the dominant and minority cultures to mingle and merge but important cherished elements of the minority culture remain distinctive. In order for a person to function effectively in a foreign country and its culture, some degree of acculturation is necessary. In assimilation, however, the subtle tendency (and sometimes it's not so subtle) is for the dominant culture to pressure immigrants in the country to adopt its values and customs. The degree to which an immigrant acculturates or assimilates is basically a personal decision. However, in the absence of guidance and support, sometimes feelings of inferiority or tensions around issues such as "not fitting in" push immigrants to choose to abandon their culture and heritage and totally assimilate into the dominant culture. When a dominant culture is not open to diversity, discriminates, and harbors expectations that persons new to the culture must assimilate, this does not support the blending of values. Worse still, this demonstrates a total lack of respect for cultural and value differences. In my humble opinion, dominant cultures that subtly and not so subtly force assimilation are poorer as a result of doing so because they are denied the richness and vibrancy that diversity brings.

This cultural "balancing act" forced upon parents of bicultural children gives rise to a whole host of parenting questions that other parents do not have to ask. What adds to the challenge is that there are so many subjective questions that are important, but we can't readily find objective answers for them. We do know, however, that finding appropriate responses to these questions is imperative because this will to a great extent influence the future of our children. For instance, should we force our children to speak our native language? Should we teach them authoritatively the values that we believe in? Should we allow them to participate in a high school prom? Should we allow them to participate in a sleepover at a friend's house? As Muslims, should we celebrate Christmas? Are we overprotective of our children? Are we being overly rigid, strict, and demanding in our child rearing practices because of our strong desire to have our children value their heritage? The list of questions could go on and on.

Because of heavy workloads and other time consuming commitments, many of us may not be able, or are unwilling, to communicate with our kids effectively or adequately, especially when they are younger. In addition to having to cope with being a minority in a dominant culture, our children also struggle with going through the various and often difficult stages in their life that all children have to go through. Effectively maneuvering through and managing these various stages is of crucial importance to our children's long-term well-being and success. In light of this, we must help them in any possible way to cope with the physical changes, the emotional ups and downs, shifting peer relationships, and sometimes volatile outbursts they may experience, especially during their teenage years.

As parents, we must make sure that our kids understand that we are not trying to control their lives, or subject them to excessive restrictions; we are not intentionally doing things or deciding things just to make them unhappy. Although our love for our children should be unconditional and undivided, teaching them the importance of responsibility and self-discipline at home, at school, and elsewhere is extremely important. They may sometimes think that our "tough love" treatment is harsh or unfair; this is when it is more important then ever that they be assured that we have their best interest in our hearts.

As bicultural children, they should also be made to understand that even though we cherish and respect the prevailing culture of this country, we have been raised in a distinctively different culture that we also deeply cherish, perhaps even more so. We are extremely proud of our native culture, and sometimes we are even obsessed with it. With this being said, we must also let them know that we have no doubt that our culture has its strengths and weakness, its good and bad attributes. All in all, we want our children to learn and to respect our distinct native cultural values as well as the core values of the American culture.

As immigrant parents, we are called upon to deal with our partially-Americanized children who may resist us any time we try to provide them with some guidance, or ask them to do something that may seem odd to them because it may not conform to prevailing American norms. If we do not embrace our responsibility as parents to guide them, the television, their classmates, the Internet, and their social clubs or groups will influence them in a way that we may deem inappropriate. When we try to teach them our native way of life, they may show no interest, or they may possibly become rebellious. Our advice, however, may serve as medicine, distasteful but nevertheless beneficial to their health. We hope that by the time they've grown up they will have come to recognize our love for them and appreciate our concerns for them.

To be sure, we certainly don't expect our children to lead exactly the same life style that we have lived in our native country or in our new country. It will be counterproductive if we try to mold our children in this way, or subject them to excessive restrictions. This will eventually make them defiant and confused. However, we are obligated to teach them the good values that are embodied in our native culture as well as the good things that are a part of other cultures. We want them to understand, for instance, that they should not harbor feelings of inferiority because they have one or both parents from another country. Or, it should not be embarrassing for them to speak another language. In fact to the contrary, speaking multiple languages gives one a distinct advantage in life and perhaps in work. We want them to learn, for instance, that they should acknowledge the presence of other people, instead of ignoring them; they should graciously recognize others by saying hello any time they encounter another. Similarly, they should show respect for their parents and other older people by being responsive to and considerate of their feelings; they should also not raise their voice when talking to them. Some parents may even believe it is necessary to some degree, to force them, for example, to learn their native language; they do this for many good reasons. It is through learning their native language that they can access a wealth of arts, literature, history, traditions, and many other of their native cultural treasures. It is the only way they can come to respect their heritage and their ancestors of whom we are so very proud. Learning one's native language may also serve to strengthen the bond between immigrant parents and their children. Our children should learn that cherishing and keeping the traditions and beliefs of their parents is the first step toward respecting and tolerating the traditions and beliefs of others.

We expect our children not only to learn our culture, but also to be able to defend it and take pride in who they are. In order to be able to do so, we need to provide them with the intellectual tools which will enable them to explore and analyze good values, as well as critique those things which are not of value. Obviously, we can't follow our children around 24/7 and check on every move they make, nor should we. The best we can do is to provide them with an aptitude and a strong set of values that help them to distinguish between right and wrong; this involves, among other things, teaching them to think independently, and to make appropriate moral and ethical decisions when the need arises. If we do all these things, we can have greater confidence that as they grow and mature, they will be well equipped to make their own good life-enhancing choices and decisions. And as hopeful and proud parents, we continue to pray that the values we instilled in them early in their lives will be, and will forever remain, a cherished part of their lifestyle and their identity.

Does Parenting Matter?

S ince arriving in this country, I am proud to say that I have been able to accomplish almost anything that I have set my mind to; however, there are three exceptions to this: making home-made bread from scratch, preventing my socks from disappearing in the washer or dryer, and perfecting the art of my parenting. The later does not, of course, imply that I am a mediocre or an ineffective parent. No, I am perhaps a reasonably successful parent in spite of definitely being obsessive about my children and my parenting. Undoubtedly, no job in the world is tougher and more imperative than parenting especially for those of us who have no choice but to constantly deal with what I call "Americanized" kids who have "you can't make me do it" mentalities. Parents are often accused by their kids of being too strict or overly concerned about their safety, education, health, and just about everything else going on in their lives. Our parenting efforts which are based on love and concern for our children are often met with words of challenge: "I am old enough; you can't tell me what to do."

I wish good parenting was a clear, precise science but it is not. Instead, it is an art having no predetermined formula that guarantees your success. Possessing wealth, position, and a college education, or employing conscientious oversight, scrutiny, and even resorting to spanking, do not make you a good parent per se. My parents were both poor and illiterate; however, they somehow managed to raise six good kids out of a total of seven! In an effort to sharpen your parenting skills, you try to explore strategies that you think might be effective and have no loopholes that could be misused by your kids. You look for effective strategies that will help you to discourage obnoxious behaviors and reward the good manners of your kids. You do everything in you power to try and guess what your kids might be up to, and develop "eyes in the back of your head" hoping they will think you are all-seeing. You also spend time and money attending professional seminars led by so-called experts who try to teach you how to become effective parents. Relax and take a deep breath; according to some researchers, your parenting efforts are not going to make much of a difference when it comes to influencing the development of your children's personality traits or ensuring their future success. This may come as a surprise to most of us because we believe parenting really matters.

Consider the following questions. Are we parents being manipulated by profit seeking entrepreneurs who try to engender fear in us in order to create a market for their products and/or services? To what extent can we really influence our children? How effective is good parenting on the future success of our kids? Are all the conflicting views offered by these so-called parenting experts confusing to you as parents? Even if parenting practices do matter, we still have to figure out what works and what doesn't work, and what aspects of our children's personality we can influence for the good.

By conducting extensive studies, behavioral researchers have been able to provide answers to these and similar questions. What is of importance in these studies is that researchers have been able to determine how much of your child's personality is due to his or her genetic make-up, and how much is acquired from the environment in which the child lives. The results of most of these studies consistently reveal that genetic factors are responsible for 50 percent of a child's personality traits. In other words, a child will exhibit certain behaviors depending on what kind of chemical is released in the brain. The other 50 percent of a child's personality traits can be influenced by a host of external factors including parenting. If these research results are true, then there is no significant correlation between how our children may behave in response to certain situations, and how much and what we teach them. No matter how hard parents try to affect their children, parental influence will obviously be overshadowed by, among other things, the powerful influences exerted upon them by their peers, friends, and what they are exposed to at school. Even if we parents are able to have an influence on our children, which element(s) of their personality is/are most influenced by us?

Based on my own observations, which albeit are limited, Iranian parents have been rather highly successful in influencing their children when it comes to their education, but only moderately successful with respect to influencing their children's behaviors. However, because a good education is a positive and key factor in shaping children's lives, it can be said that Iranian parents have done a good job of raising their kids. Because we believe education has been the most promising road to our own success, we focus earnestly on our kids' education and rightfully so. While the link between parenting practices and the formation of a child's personality traits cannot be precisely tested because these things cannot be quantified objectively, the correlation between our kids' academic success at school and our parenting efforts can be verified by utilizing concrete statistics.

Dr. Steven Levitt, the lead author of the best selling book *Freakonomics*, has used the comprehensive data provided by the U.S. Department of Education and the Early Childhood Longitudinal Study program (ECLS) to examine the correlation between parenting and the academic success of school children. The ECLS program collects extensive data on a wide range of variables such as family, school, community, as well as individual variables such as children's intellectual development, early learning, and the kids' performance in school. Dr. Levitt has fed the data provided by ECLS through economists' most favorite statistical technique called *regression analysis* to test the correlation between a host of factors representing parenting and academic success of young kids. His findings are startling.

The academic success of children is evidently related to wide variety of factors with parenting being only one among many. Only a trained analyst using controlled experiments can measure the effect of a single factor such as parenting. Fortunately, ECLS provides comprehensive information on many factors as the proxies for parenting, sixteen of them to be exact. After extensive examination of these factors by Dr. Levitt, it turned out that only half of these factors play a significant role in students' academic success. Factors that have a significant positive influence on children's success are: the level of education of the parents, the socioeconomic status of the parents, whether parents speak English at home, the parents' involvement in Parent Teacher Associations (PTAs), how many books the parents have in the home, and the age of the mother when the first child was born. The two factors that have a significant negative impact on the child's success at school are a child's low birth weight, and whether the child lives with its biological parents or is adopted. The eight factors that have no statistically significant impact on a child's academic success are: moving to a better neighborhood, whether the child's family has remained intact, whether the mother works outside the home, whether the child attends a Head Start program, whether parents take the child to educational places such as museums, how often the child watches TV, whether parents read to the child on a regular basis, and whether the child is spanked.

It is not easy to come up with justifications for some of these findings because most of them are really complicated and certainly beyond the intended scope of my purpose in writing this as a parent. I leave the debate open and encourage your further reflection.

If you consider yourself to be an overly-concerned parent as I consider myself to be, you may find some of these results disappointing, counterintuitive, and unacceptable, and I totally agree with you. However, be advised that experimental research studies are like milling machines in that the type of "flour" you get out of them depends upon the type of "grain" you put into them. These results prove my own theory which has been built upon my own experience of raising three delightful children who are all grown up now, and are very productive, positively contributing members of society. My theory simply advises you to continue to do all the parenting you want, but know that realistically you can have only limited success when it comes to changing or influencing your kids. Furthermore, the ECLS data shows that *what you do* as a parent is not going to drastically change or influence your children's future success; however, *who you are* can have a profound influence.

As you face these many parenting challenges, my advice to you is to not give up trying. It is also important to remember that your kids' academic test scores may not be the only determinants of the kind of people they will become and the kind of success they will have when they are adults. There are many smart crooks, but there are also many not-so-clever but decent honestly productive people in the world. The happiness of your children and the kind of life style they will eventually have may not be totally dependent on their intellectual capabilities alone.

I will end by offering you another very important piece of advice; refrain from using spanking as a parenting practice. Not only is it totally ineffective, it often shows your children just how bankrupt and powerless you are as a parent. In the short term, spanking may stop disruptive behavior, but in the long term this does not elicit respect from your children; quite often, it does just the opposite. Also, you are providing bad modeling of how human beings should interact with one another when in conflict. The violent behavior of parents most often breeds violent behavior in their children. Learn all that you can learn about good parenting, but most importantly, teach your children and love them in ways that leave them with behaviors and attitudes that reflect the power of respect, patience, understanding, and learned wisdom.

A Letter to My Son

My Dear Son,

I decided to write you this letter on the occasion of your 20th birthday because I believe you are now mature enough to have a good understanding of the world around you. Plus, I wanted to give you concrete expression of a gift that you cannot buy at any store at any price, the gift of love, admiration, and support.

You will graduate from university in a couple of years and will soon be ready to take on the challenges and the responsibilities of the real world. You will have to make some tough decisions concerning your education, your career, and other important matters in your life. As you know, important decisions are not easy and sometimes they are cumbersome to make.

Your mother and I have always been with you from the moment you were born and have always been there for you whenever you needed support, guidance, protection, and assistance in any way. In our Iranian culture, children mean a lot to a family. They are the pride and the joy of the family and life's most precious assets. We love you unconditionally, and are committed to do whatever it takes to help you excel and lead a happy and prosperous life. You have, thus far, fulfilled all of our expectations above and beyond what we had hoped for. We have been utterly proud of you and your accomplishments up until now and definitely we will be proud of you in the future. Despite the fact that we love you so dearly, we may often fail to put our love into words, spoken or written, or other forms of affectionate expression. It is just that the emotionally reserved nature of our native culture precludes us sometimes from expressing our love for our kids easily, warmly, and candidly. We can only hope that this has not prevented you from feeling the true love we have for you.

Although you are an intelligent young man, we believe it is important for us to continue to provide guidance and support for you especially when it comes to certain important matters. There are some things in life that come best with age and experience. We understand that you may occasionally consider our concerns to be over blown, unnecessary, or even embarrassing. However, expressing concern is an integral part of being successful parents. Have no doubt that we have always had your best interests in our hearts. I remember, sometimes we had frenzied arguments with you, but unhearing lecturing was not our intent. On rare occasions we may have spanked you, but no physical harm was intended. We may have irritated you by comparing you to your older brother or sister, but no denigration was in our minds. We have always loved you just the way you are.

I remember when I was a kid I always relied on my parents and on my older brothers and sisters; they were the most trustworthy sources of consultation and comfort. Although my parents were strict disciplinarians and correct in their own judgment, they were also very considerate. I completely understood that and tried not to do anything that would hurt their feelings. Although none of the members of my family have formal education—most of them cannot even sign their names—they are very knowledgeable about life's important matters. My parents did not do for me any of the things that modern parents do for their children. I don't remember that they ever drove me to school, bought me a toy, took me to a restaurant, or spent any so-called quality time with me. But they were good parents, the best, and that is what matters. As a traditional poor farmer, my father had to work hard every day for many long hours. He did not have any additional time to spend with me. If I needed love and affection, I always could turn to my mother. My high respect for both of them did not allow me to challenge their decisions, be dismissive of their feelings, or even to raise my voice when talking to them. I thought, and I still think, that I had the best parents in the whole world, and I never felt that I needed better ones. Now that I am a parent, what else could I expect from my children except what my parents expected from me?

The abundance you take for granted today, was for me an attainable luxury that I had to work very hard for when I was your age. I was about twenty-four years old when I came to this country as a young ambitious student, just like you, motivated by curiosity and in search of a better life. My decision to come to the United States was totally my own. I remember I had a dark brown suitcase in my right hand, a dictionary in my left hand, $2,100 in my pocket, and a burning desire in my heart to succeed. As a bewildered novice in a totally strange land, I knew nobody that I could turn to, had no experience to draw on, and could barely speak English. From the onset of my journey to this country, I had to work hard because I knew that was the only way for me to support myself and to continue my education. I had to do odd jobs ranging from janitoring, car hopping, dishwashing, truck driving, and pizza delivering to support myself and my education. I did them all. Did I like them? No. I hated them but I didn't have much choice. I did not let the feeling of despair overwhelm me. I considered those odd jobs as the temporary sources of income that I needed to support my long-term goal which was to have a good education. Surviving might be easy; succeeding is not. I managed to climb my way up inch by inch through perseverance and hard work. This is not to claim that I am an immensely successful person, but given the circumstances, I think I have done very well. I am not dissatisfied or disappointed with my life in any way.

You see, the world we live in may not be as simple as it looks, or as we think it is. You may not have seen enough of it yet. They say that whatever a young man sees in a mirror, an old person sees on a bare wall. Your heart is like a shiny, spotless mirror that shows everything nicely and clearly. You certainly see what is happening today; however, you may not be farsighted enough to see what may come about in the distant future. You can rely on your intellectual ability for academic matters. There are, however, some important things that come to us best with age and with experience. As your parents and as people with extensive experience in life, we envision your future, and we want it to be as bright and productive as possible. To secure such a prosperous future, we need to invest in it now. I know that it is difficult to work hard and pass all those classes with good grades, but learning is not always fun. Sometimes good things like a good medicine may not be tasty to swallow, but they are certainly useful and often life saving for us.

I know many things may happen everyday that we may not like or do not approve. But remember, we cannot control everything. Therefore, we should not allow uncontrollable events distract us, because if we do, we let them control our life. Sometimes, we may also be treated unfairly or be discriminated against. However, we should overcome such treatment through determination and the quality of our work, and move on. Time is the best healer. You need to be patient. Sometimes things have to go through their natural course. To me, life is like a moving chart; it may be forced to fluctuate up and down in the short run but maintains its steady upward trend in the long run.

My dear son, by the time you graduate from university, I am sure there will still be crimes committed by some social misfits; there will be war and other catastrophic events; many families may still be left behind when it comes to health, education, and other social service; many will still die from AIDS and heart attacks everyday; there will be continuing clashes and ethnic cleansing in different parts of the world; there may still be lingering fear of economic recession; the Federal Reserve may still be struggling to successfully pump more liquidity into the economy; poverty and famine will not yet be eradicated. In spite of all this, I am optimistic that you will launch your career in a much better world than the one in which I started mine.

Forever, Love You, Dad

Are We Worried About the Wrong Things?

As we all witnessed, the decade of the 1990s was an era of many wide-ranging triumphs for the U.S. economy. Growing affluence strongly indentified this period of time. Massive investment in highly innovative information systems technology triggered the proliferation of high tech businesses and the emergence of e-commerce that paved the way for an impending surge in productivity and growth. Moreover, the United States was the major beneficiary of the monumental events that took place in the 90s such as the disintegration of the former Soviet Union and the fall of the Berlin wall. These events gave the United States the opportunity to cut its military spending and devote more of its resources to fuel its economic development. Prolonged economic progress and growth, accompanied by low unemployment and low inflation, led to a tremendous accumulation of wealth and increasing income. The growth rate of the U.S. Gross Domestic Product (GDP) reached its peak during the 90s. While only 4.5

percent of the world's population lived in the U.S., her share of the world GDP grew to 24 percent of the world's total Gross Domestic Product during this period. This rate, of course, has been slightly but steadily declining since then. A few emerging countries have been able to achieve persistent high economic growth in recent years, and threaten to unseat the United States as the sole economic superpower. Despite this competition, the United States has to this point in time managed to remain the dominant economic as well as political power in the world.

U. S. economic progress, however, may give us as citizens a false sense of contentment, security, and human well-being. It is tempting to think that materialistic progress will also enhance our overall level of welfare and promote social justice. I think we are more skeptical now about the automatic connection between material growth and growth in our overall level of well-being; evidence may even point to the contrary. A growing number of people in the United States, for instance, do not necessarily enjoy a more peaceful and worry-free life despite their material progress and higher standard of living. Fear and anxiety, often triggered by our inability to fulfill our inflated worldly expectations, are prevalent feelings that are growing and taking over the life of American consumers. Fear and its resulting psychological disorders seem to have become severe and ubiquitous. More noticeably, these often unfounded fears have been created by greedy entrepreneurs and injudicious politicians, and are reinforced by mass communication media. Dubious fear, fear of something that may not even happen, or may not ever have a chance of happening, is infinitesimal. Mental distresses, the offshoot of fears, seem to have reached epic proportions in this country. Psychiatric drugs such as Prozac, Paxil, and Zoloft are among the top 15 most prescribed medications with annual sales amounting to about $10 billion. Prozac is designed to relieve a person from anxiety and fear; Paxil is designed for those of us who fear social gatherings and have no desire or courage to deal with other people.

Who can forget the Y2K (year 2000 date turnover for computers) fear that the computer savvy professionals engendered, stoked, and tried to sell to ordinary people? Americans were warned by "experts" for well over a year to expect something like Armageddon. In preparation for this dire event, many converted the basements of their homes into storehouses of food and other necessities because they were led to believe that life as we once knew it would be in absolute chaos. Numerous companies, institutions of all sorts, as well as the American government, spent millions of dollars trying to anticipate and prepare for dealing with the perceived catastrophic computer-related consequences of the Y2K turnover. As we all remember well, the first day of the year 2000 started and ended just as any other day. Nothing out of the ordinary happened. There were no disruptions in electricity, water, or communication networks. There were no major breakdowns of computer networks. No missiles were launched by hostile enemies, and no airplanes crashed to the ground. In summary, water did not move from water! *Ab as ab takan nakhord* as Persians would say. All those who spent so much time, so much money, and so many resources in preparation for the imaginary disasters were disappointed; thus, the resources expended in preparation were considered wasted. That experience by itself indicated that even though we are vulnerable to technological calamities, we are not as much controlled by them as we might think. Yet, we did not learn enough from that experience to keep us from still capitulating to the efforts of those who try to capitalize on our fears, apprehensions, and vulnerability.

Some of us may hesitate to leave our homes because we are fearful that something may happen to us. The sources of our fears are endless but let me highlight a few. We are worried about global warming, or getting sick from consuming tainted tomatoes, peanut-based products, and recalled beef. We worry that saturated fats may block our arteries. We worry that our kids may be shot at school or become victims of other random acts of violence. We worry that our personal physical health might be jeopardized by all or one of the following: a deadly fall on the stairs, being hit by a chunk of ice or other debris falling from sky, getting sick from consuming genetically-altered food, contracting the West Nile virus, getting cancer from artificial sweeteners and a host of other suspicious products like toxic baby bottles and other plastic containers we use in our everyday life. I would be negligent if I did not also mention the ever-present worries about possibly being audited by IRS, and the possibility that we might become victims of terrorist attacks in the future.

While a number of these fears may have some validity and we should be prepared to protect ourselves and manage them, there are more irrational fears that are often exploited and turned into money-making schemes. We are often fearful of the wrong things mainly because our risk assessment mechanism is often erroneous, or our ability to winnow credible information from rumor is weak. Our subjective feelings will usually lead us to imprecise or sometimes mistaken conclusions.

Where do all of these unfounded fears come from?

Given the fact that many biased experts, ill-intentioned politicians, and profit-seeking entrepreneurs pitch their cleverly crafted exploitive agendas with great gusto, it becomes very easy for us to react irrationally to faulty information as well as to unfounded rumors. For instance, despite what some politicians want us to believe, we are not living in an increasingly dangerous world. Let's step back and take a calm, rational look at some facts. Violence, organized crime activity, and terrorist attacks have subsided in recent years. In the wake of 9/11, Jihadist's (the term invented in the U.S. to refer to Islamic fundamentalists) sometimes fanatic activity and the fear this engenders has not proven to be catastrophic. The risk of becoming a victim of Internet fraud has been vastly exaggerated. As yet, no one has died from mad cow disease or avian influenza. However, we organize and agonize over these and similar fears; overreaction has become the norm rather than the exception. An example of this overreaction is comparing the powerless president of Iran, Mahmoud Ahmadi Nejad, to Hitler. This was President Bush's frivolous attempt to portray Iran as a major threat to world peace despite the fact that Iran poses no threat, and is incapable of posing such a threat to the U.S. or to the West. If there is one thing that some US politicians are good at, it is blowing things out of proportion. They are shrewd marketers of fear disguised as politicians.

Unsuspecting and over protective parents are among the primary targets of the so-called scaremongering experts which are a fast-growing species in this country. We have too many after-the-fact experts who are so sure of themselves. These overly confident experts usually are merely seeking attention and the public spotlight by insisting on and promoting their one-sided, often extreme views. They are supposedly providing professional advice; however, in actuality they do nothing but spread fear. They utilize fear tactics to influence our decisions and create high public emotion which is not necessarily compatible with rationality. They often manipulate or misuse statistics to serve their own self-interests with the ultimate goal of creating a market and earning profits for themselves. We are all vulnerable to exploitation by these so-called experts, especially overly concerned and gullible parents. They use our unfounded fears and our aversion to taking risks against us. When it comes to advice about what to do and what not to do in raising our kids, we will be easily persuaded to do just about anything because we think that if we make a mistake, the consequences will be calamitous both financially and emotionally. We also abhor the thought that others may label us "bad parents" if we do not capitulate to the current thinking and fads regarding child rearing.

Fear-mongering is a lucrative business in the U.S. and too often it is the secret of economic survival for some companies. Briefly stated, in market-based economies, profit is the only incentive for economic initiatives. In order to turn a profit, businessmen have to be able to sell. In order to sell, there has to be a strong sustained demand for their products. What do they do if the market is saturated and potential demand is lacking? When this happens, they are forced to resort to their imaginative creativity; sometimes this creativity is levelheaded, but all too often it is senseless. They try to exploit every possible means to create demand and the right conditions that are conducive to manipulation. How many more brands of SUVs do we need? What other sophisticated features we can add to a cell phone? How many more flavors of ice cream can we scream for? What other vitamins we can add to a bottle of water? How many more calories can we remove from frozen foods and still have them be edible products? We spend billions of dollars producing, amending, marketing, and selling fear-relief products that are not even marginally life-enhancing; in addition, these products become ineffective very quickly. In the United States, we spend billions of dollars on the purchase, maintenance, and monitoring of safety and detection devices in places like schools despite the fact that schools are still the safest places for children. The odds of your child drowning in your neighbor's swimming pool are probably higher then the odds of your child getting shot at school. Nonetheless, we are more afraid of the danger at school than the danger of a swimming pool.

The public media plays a significant role in creating and spreading irrational fear. News is spread throughout the world very quickly and likewise, the fear that the news may generate. We live in fear of terrorist attacks when the news media report a terrorist attack on a remote island we may never have heard of before; we hear about an airplane crash in a third word country and it creates fear despite the fact that air travel is still the safest mode of transportation. The widespread use of the Internet has also spread another type of fear; we fear online identity theft and the fraudulent use of your vital personal or financial information. Now, many are trying to jump on the band wagon, seeking to convince you that protecting your personal information on the Internet is as important as insuring your home for flood, fire, and other catastrophic events. Even colleges and universities are offering courses and certificates designed to help you manage or minimize online risk, and how to protect yourself from becoming a victim of online financial fraud. In my view, all you need to do to safeguard your vital personal information is to be more careful.

I believe it is the nature of human beings that when our basic needs are taken care of and there is no need to worry about food and shelter, we create other things to be anxious about. This theory of fears and accompanying worry is similar to psychologist Abraham Maslow's theory called *The Hierarchy of Needs*. The first level of need is basic physiological needs (food, shelter, clothing) followed by safety needs, then social needs, and finally, the need for self-esteem. So, once we no longer have to worry about food and shelter, we become free to worry about higher level things. These higher level worries and anxieties could arise from our thinking of the possibility that we may become unable to maintain the standard of living to which we have become accustom, or the possibility that we may not be able to fulfill our overblown expectations. In other words, when basic needs are satisfied, the worry associated with them evaporates. In keeping with the saying "Nature abhors a vacuum," we then tend to fill this "worry vacuum" with higher level needs that have fears associated with them. We search deep inside ourselves to find rationalizations for our fears. This tendency seems to be innate and hardwired into our brain. We always find excuses to worry, especially during good times. When economic conditions are favorable, the causes and sources of fear seem to multiply. The economic materialistic progress we have made in recent decades in the U.S. has created all sorts of anxieties, especially because this progress has led to increasing inequality and a skewed distribution of wealth. The rich keep getting richer and the poor keep getting poorer. This ever widening income gap between the "haves" and "have-nots" will eventually become a problem that we will have to deal with; if we do not deal with this gap, it will lead to deep economic recession because of its adverse effects on the middle class. The middle class, which has been so important to our economic stability, could eventually disappear.

All of these reflections on the subject of worry remind me of our own cute Farsi expression: (*ghorbane khodam ke khar naaram, as ka va jovash khabar nadaram*), Lucky me, I don't have a donkey, so I don't need to worry about the (cost of) donkey food!

In Monica We Seek Profit

We are obsessed with many things in our lives; the healthier obsession is with our kids. We often brag about them stridently. We take pride in their successes, particularly in education and in their careers. We claim, for instance, that they earn more than we do. But do they really? Not according to some researchers including Matt Miller, the author of a very intriguing book entitled *The Tyranny of the Dead Ideas*. In his book he explains how, above all, the current economic crisis has changed our collective perception of many axiomatic ideas such as the idea that there is a cause and effect link between economic success and one's aptitude. America as a nation seems to be moving toward a dangerous socioeconomic duality because of a skewed reward system under which certain groups undeservingly reap the benefits of our free enterprise system while others are left behind. It is greed that is changing the milieu of our culture.

In particular, America's current economic calamity has especially exposed the unfairness of the corporate compensation scheme, and how the perceived link between CEO compensation and performance is nothing but a myth. Our current economic crisis has revealed that many CEOs have been rewarded handsomely by their boards of directors despite their dismal performance and their unethical behavior. While the poor performance of some CEOs and their unethical behavior is what has gotten us into this economic mess, corporate compensation practices continue to make some of these CEOs very rich very quickly. The average annual compensation of a CEO in the United States is at least 36 times larger than the average earnings of an ordinary employee who works for the CEO's company. What kind of disincentive effects do such revelations have for ordinary people like you and me who try to climb our way up the economic ladder through hard work and perseverance? The sad realization is that having a good college education and struggling uphill no longer matter in this country when it comes to earning income and respect. My fear is that this sad state of affairs may eventually lead ordinary Americans to pessimistic thinking and erode their faith in the free market system. To tell the truth, I think this has already occurred. Devaluation of the work ethic and resulting inertia has created a sense of mediocrity in most of our kids. This mediocrity is especially evidenced by the belief of young people that they can gain a college degree, for example, with minimum intellectual effort, and by their general inability or unwillingness to work hard for a good education. In the experience of most of us, especially immigrant families, parents are more educated than their kids. Our kids have been lured into so many frivolous, time-wasting activities that they have no time left to devote to decent learning and solid education.

In order to try to make sense out of what is happening in our country and with our young people, I fantasized an experiment. A group of indolent people were placed in a hot sauna room. The goal was to find out which of these individuals were the laziest. The experimenters started gradually raising the temperature in the sauna and monitored the reactions of the people inside. After a while, a few of the people who didn't want to take the excessive heat started to object and left the room. A few of the group, who were apparently lazier than the indolent people who had left, remained in the room. Of those who remained, some did object verbally, however, they didn't move physically; the rest of them said "Why don't you object on our behalf too." The people who asked this question were the ones who were crowned as the laziest of all in the sauna because they didn't even care enough to raise their own voices. Even though this is a fictional story, it is meant to remind us of a somber problem and provides an image of what is going on especially with the youth of America. They are a perplexed generation that is deteriorating over time and we are not doing anything about it. Some would label them as "Generation X" because they are as unknown as the "X" in mathematical equations. The letter X has always been the symbol for an unknown variable in mathematics, just as this generation is unknown to many of us.

Based on my first-hand prolonged experience with young people as an educator, I have come to believe that many of our youth are becoming lazy, unmotivated, disinterested, and approach life with a much too easy-going mentality. They can't be bothered to raise their voices despite the fact that they are burning in a hot sauna-like environment. This generation has become the captives of materialism and its profiteering operators who are manipulating and exploiting it for material gain.

To make matters worse, we shamelessly glorify abhorrent behaviors. We may remember the story of Monica Lewinsky, a story that kept us occupied for many years. Monica was a young woman who worked in the White House as an intern. Sometime during the course of her tenure as an intern, she successfully seduced the forty-second President of the United States, and was able to engage him in a tawdry extramarital sexual relationship. After years of successfully keeping the affair a secret from the American public, the "fairy-tale" story eventually exploded in a shameful way, and brought disgrace to the office of the presidency and to the reputation of this nation. The whole political establishment was embarrassed. The story was so bizarre that politicians had no choice but to impeach the president. Undoubtedly, if this kind of presidential behavior took place in an Eastern country, the public would be outraged and reactions would be much more swift and aggressive. Maybe Eastern politicians who could not bear the shame extramarital affairs of elected officials bring upon their countries would take more drastic measures to punish the guilty party. But, "East is East and West is West."

For years Monica was one of the best known celebrities in this country and she profited substantially from her reprehensible behavior. In an effort to capitalize on her fame, greedy entrepreneurs jumped on the band wagon and tried to cash in; they wanted "to bake bread before the oven got cold" so to speak. They offered Monica lucrative contracts, including one involving a book about her story. She was like life-saving food in a time of famine; everyone wanted a piece of the action. The book was a best seller for a time, owing to heavy promotion by the publisher, the media frenzy that surrounded her, and the public's insatiable appetite for sensational junk. Many business firms didn't want to be left out and tried to catch some valuable fish in this golden pond. They vied for her attention and her signature on their contracts. Jenny Craig, for instance, offered Monica one million dollars in exchange for her appearance on its TV commercials, and becoming a spokeswoman for the company. Stories like that are not things of the past. You may become outraged when you hear stories like this today and you should be. One million dollars is equivalent to more than twenty-five years worth of salary for a seasoned school teacher. What has become of our values and priorities as a country?

Following this some years later, the ousted governor of Illinois, Rod Blagojevich, signed a book deal which offered him a six figure payment in exchange for the publication of his forthcoming book.

Such deals are becoming shamelessly customary in this country. People, especially famous people, are profiting from their crimes and malicious deeds. When ordinary people commit a crime they end up in jail. But if you are a well-known public figure you write a book and make millions off of your crime, which in my mind is a crime in itself. Why is this happening? It's happening because publicity is one of the most precious commodities in this economy; whether positive or negative, it really doesn't matter. Publicity has the potential to generate big money for all involved. Many companies sought to profit from Monica's story and they did so successfully. They unlimitedly enriched their coffers just as some of those CEOs who forced this nation's economy into its current turmoil enriched their coffers. Where is the shame and when will we learn to stand up and put a stop to this unconscionable greed?

One million dollars was a handsome reward for Monica who should personally be really embarrassed and publicly ostracized. But what we have done instead as a society is reward her for what she had done. I have no qualms about the notion that a market economy works because it is based on incentives. But, should we let it take us in any silly and perhaps destructive direction? Should our society allow individuals like Monica benefit from their ignominy? The profit-seeking entrepreneurs stand in line to meet her and to strike a deal with her. Not only was she not punished, she was compensated for her despicable behavior. She took advantage of the political and economic systems of this country, and with the help of a group of equally money-conscious lawyers, was able to turn her misdeeds into a fortune for herself and others. Who would have thought that a naïve young girl could get so close to the president of the most powerful nation on the face of earth? Who could have thought that the President of the United States, who is supposedly the most powerful man in the world, would have such a weak state of mind and morality which allowed him to justify his whims and those of a young girl?

What kind of image is being projected by these stories? Are we omitting the word "shame" from our vocabulary? Are we telling and demonstrating to our younger generation that education, hard work, and honesty will get them nowhere? Are we teaching our young people that they will make more money cutting corners, looking for a free-ride, and engaging in inappropriate or even criminal deeds, than they will through hard work and living and deciding with personal moral integrity? How can we expect to sustain and strengthen moral codes in a society that rewards and even glorifies crimes? It should be repugnant to the people of this country to allow its moral values to be overshadowed by, or even defeated in confrontation with, the profiteering endeavors of a bunch of self-serving entrepreneurs. It is even more regrettable when individuals like Monica become role models for many young people who may be enticed to follow her example.

As I ponder further on my fictionalized experiment, I realize that I don't know if or when the lazy people of the story will ultimately move and come to their senses. I also worry that they will become dehydrated, brittle, and eventually break because the room they are in is too hot.

To All the Students I Have Taught: Fun with Economics

Scientists may have expensive solutions to life's small problems; economists offer inexpensive solutions to life's big problems.

Who said economics is a dismal science? For me for the most part, it makes pleasant commonsense. Economics is practiced and economic decisions are made every day by people. This happens in simple ways like when you shop at the supermarket, borrow money to finance the purchase of a house or an automobile, decide how many courses you will take next semester, decide whether to buy or rent a place of residence, and even when you decide whether to commit a crime or not! You try to beat the stock market when you invest your money smartly. You don't need to be told that saving money, searching for good deals, investing wisely and increasing your finances is good for you. You don't need to be told that you should strive to raise your standard of living. You don't need to be reminded that you need the basic necessities such as food, shelter, clothes, medical expenses and other basic necessities. These and other needs are physiologically innate, and utilizing effective economic tools can help meet and satisfy these basic needs.

When I was an elementary school kid, my family owned a milking cow that served us well as a supplementary source of income for our household. The cow was big and fat, and we got many good monetary offers from our neighborhood butchers who wanted to buy and slaughter the innocent animal for its meat. My father steadfastly refused to accept these offers. Even though my father was an illiterate man, he was smart enough to know that you should not sell or kill a milking cow. It made more long term economic sense to let the cow continue to give milk and generate income for our family every day.

I know you have often complained about the "abstract" nature of economic analyses. The best explanation I can give for this abstractness is that economics is not a vocational-type subject that provides you with a concrete set of readily available tools from a toolbox. Instead, economics is a way of thinking; it's a way of thinking about and applying economic concepts, principles, theories, and understanding interrelated dynamics. The benefits of being economically savvy and wise come to you in the long run when you become someone who has to make important economic decisions, decisions that literally have costly consequences. But wait a minute; don't blow off being concerned for your future just because you may be saying to yourselves, "In the long run, aren't we all dead, retired, or deported back to our home countries?" And also while we are on the subject of the abstract and concrete nature of things, let me give you another piece of helpful advice. If you like the kids who live on your block, let them know that you like them only in the abstract and not in the concrete. If you don't, they may come and mess up your freshly-poured concrete driveway!

I have tried to teach you the *Law of Diminishing Marginal Utility*. But I often ask myself if this law will ever become operational for my wife in my lifetime. I invite you to come and see the basement, the garage, and the many walk-in closets in my house. These places are all stuffed with shoes, purses, women's clothes, and all sorts of other unwanted items. My wife has not even used many of these things for years, and many other things are brand new items with the sale tags still on them. And just between you and me, these are not the only things in our house my wife has not used for many years! The law of diminishing marginal utility never applies to her insatiable appetite for shopping and collecting. If it is on sale, she buys it. Sometimes I think she is the only reason why the Keynesian spending multiplier remains fully operational! She has an endless desire to buy things, many of which are never used or they are rarely used; eventually these things just become household annoyances. The things my wife buys eventually find their way to AMVETS stores, the Salvation Army, or to Thrift Shops. If there was an Oscar or some other major award for the most generous contributor to these organizations, it would certainly be awarded to her. I also wonder when the law of diminishing marginal utility will become operational for my teen age son who never gets tired of buying electronic games, Pokémon cards, *Star Wars* memorabilia, Happy Meals, toys, and the crummy stuff offered online. I doubt that the law of diminishing marginal utility applies to my rich friend either. He once invited my family to his birthday party and told us not to bring him any presents. And, as we were leaving the party, he asked us to take something from his house because he was fed up with all the unwanted things he had accumulated. With all due respect Jeremy Bentham (1748-1832), I think it is time to honorably retire the law of diminishing marginal utility!

As you have learned, classical economists keep telling us that the market economy works best if it is left to its own forces such as supply, demand, profit, costs, etc. Monetary forces, if they are not disturbed or tampered with, are capable of guiding consumers, investors, and entrepreneurs as they work toward making optimal economic decisions. Modern economies are supposed to work like a smart computer that has built-in sophisticated mechanisms capable of detecting most of its irregularities automatically and rectifying them. The advocates of this idea warn us about the awful consequences that will befall us if these built-in economic stabilizers are disturbed by the interference of uninformed sources like the government. Unwanted outcomes will ensue only if the laws of economics are infringed upon, the laws of demand and supply are ignored, or fundamental economic principles are overlooked.

The marvel of this market economy enables you go to mega supermarkets every day and find there almost anything that you would want. There is enough food for the over 300 million people who live in the United States. In this country, we have never heard of persistent food shortages or destabilizing surpluses. Imagine your son who just graduated from college asking you to buy him a car; there would be hundreds of different models available to him. Or if your company suddenly transfers you to another town, city, or even another state, you will have no problem in your new place of residence quickly finding housing, food, and all the other things that you're used to buying. There are plenty of products in this country waiting to be purchased. What magic forces can establish such a delicate coordination between endless human desires and the available means to fulfill them? What prevents the formation of persistent surpluses, shortages, and bottlenecks? How are all of the seemingly unrelated decisions that are made every day by millions of individual entrepreneurs coordinated? What influences the decisions of businessmen and industries to produce digital cameras, computers, paper clips, appliances for your house, digital converter boxes for your televisions, fuel for your automobile, software for your computer, and low calorie soft drinks or beers to complement your pizza? The answer to all of these questions is *the market*. The market is a well-organized, well established system that coordinates all of the economic activities that we take for granted.

The phrase "invisible hands" is one of the most cherished metaphors coined by Adam Smith, the founder of modern economics (again, no relation to the late Anna Nicole Smith!). He popularized this phrase more than two hundred years ago. It is designed to insinuate the notion that individuals are guided by their own self-interests when making economic choices. In the process of pursuing their own self-interests, enterprising individuals will also create desirable outcomes for society in the form of useful products. You can see every day how individually initiated activities, which are propelled by self interest, are synchronized by market forces. It is utterly foolish to think that farmers grow wheat, or butchers supply meat, or publishers print books for you because they are motivated by altruistic reasons and moved by philanthropic feelings. While they might be concerned about your welfare, it is high profit margins and self-interest that inspire them to do what they do. This is perfectly legitimate and acceptable as long as they do not get too greedy or resort to deceptive practices.

You know that economists do it at the margin! You know that elasticity of demand is like the length of the rubber band on your pajama. The fatter you become, the longer the waistband stretches because of the pressure exerted on it by your bulging stomach! Although you may not be familiar with the concept of consumer surplus, you surely understand that in a market economy consumers are sovereign and they rule. They decide what kind of solutions should be applied to solve life's most basic economic problems.

The government should not disturb the forces of the market that guide consumers. Let the government performs any necessary adjustments but only when citizen's demand that it does so. You know that government assistance is needed only in extreme cases when the country's economic situation is really in bad shape. As the saying goes, "If it is not broken, don't fix it." I once quipped in response to my neighbor who was soliciting my advice, "If you are not constipated, why do you want to take laxitives?" You may know the difference between fixed costs and variable costs. You've also heard of U-shaped average costs. But I bet you haven't heard of, or don't care about, or don't calculate opportunity costs. People are fooled by the notion that if something does not cost them any money, it is free; it is not really free. Even if something is free monetarily, it usually involves some kind of sacrifice or "hidden costs." I often see an ad in my favorite newspaper *Penny Saver*. The ad offers free stuff; one time it advertized a piano. The piano itself is free. However, this "free offer" may require you to pay for gas to drive somewhere to pick the piano up; you may have to pay to rent a truck to transport the piano to your house; you may have to pay for special equipment to move the piano; or, you may have to get help from friends or family members. In the end, all of this costs you valuable time as well as money.

Remember one day in class I explained the benefits of free trade based on the *Law of Comparative Advantage,* and how it is mutually beneficial for all parties involved. The benefits, however, may not be evenly divided between the parties. So be advised, this rule especially does not apply to *romance*. Because men are more eager for romance, they have weaker bargaining power when negotiating with their wives or girlfriends!

I know sometimes you may get frustrated with the proliferation of the varieties of products from which to choose; this large number of choices can really make your life more complicated. There is no end to the extravagant race to produce irresponsible product differentiation. We produce massively. The modern economic marketplace has become oversaturated with choices of product ornamentation, accessories, and additives. More than 70 models of SUVs are offered to consumers as well as more than 31 flavors of ice cream. Add to this countless assortments of laundry detergent, toothpaste, shampoo, dental floss, frozen foods, beer and soft drinks; the examples I could give are endless. It seems that in markets saturated with luxury amenities, inventiveness is the secret to survival. Manufacturers try desperately to outdo one another. We are offered fancy cell phones equipped with a myriad of functions: animated screens, picture-taking capabilities, electronic games, text messaging, Internet access, and many other features most consumers neither desire nor have the talent to use. We have forgotten that the original function of a telephone was to enable the user to make audio calls to other people; the purpose was not taking pictures and certainly not playing games. Each fancy phone comes with a *User Guide* loaded with instructions that make us feel like dummies because we are unable to understand or follow the directions. The proliferation of food product choices with their minute differentiations cause us to spend an inordinate amount of time in supermarkets; we read and compare labels in our desperate search for a wise choice of vitamin, fat, carbohydrate, sugar, calorie, cholesterol, sodium, and protein content. After my brief review of all this "progress," imagine how many psychological problems we have already created for ourselves because we cannot fulfill our inflated expectations, and how many more problems we will create for ourselves in the future. Imagine the number of stress factors we have introduced into our lives that may have adverse affects on our physical health now, and the increased adverse physical consequences if we continue this pattern into the future. As the saying goes, "It's a great life if you don't weaken!"

By the way, to those of you who bring your fancy cell phone into the men's locker room in my health club, I plead with you not to jeopardize my privacy by taking pictures of me unclothed; leave something for me to brag about personally!

Finally, as I have often told you amusingly in class, a course in economics is like a *Martha Stewart* television show; it teaches you something new every day. At the end of the last semester, I was speaking with one of my students who would be graduating soon. I extended to him my congratulations on his achievement and said, "You are graduating. Can you tell me what the most important thing was that you learned in my classes?" He replied proudly, "Well, I learned which way is vertical and which way is horizontal! Thanks to you Mr. Varjavand!"

Endorsements

F luent and easy to read, Reza Varjavand's first non-academic book, *From Misery Alley to Missouri Valley*, contains a delightful collection of informative, thought-provoking, honest, and witty stories of his life. Based on his nearly four decades of living in America, Varjavand reflects on a wide range of issues related to Iranian culture, American culture, Islam, relationships, parenting, stereotyping, discrimination, and transitioning from a traditional Iranian culture to a new American culture and way of life. Written in a highly frank and personal manner, Varjavand takes you through an unforgettable intercultural journey that will simultaneously makes you laugh, learn, and sympathize with the multitude of cultural challenges faced by an Iranian immigrant. I highly recommend this illuminating, funny, real, and generally lighthearted memoir to all Iranian-American and other hyphenated and non-hyphenated expatriates in America and elsewhere.

Yahya R. Kamalipour, PhD

Professor, Author, and Editor

Professor Varjavand writes the compelling story of a poor rural Iranian boy with illiterate parents who defies the odds by becoming a successful Economics professor in Chicago. His story is a captivating tale of Iranian rural customs and the fight to fulfill a dream. He is an inspiration for all who have come to this country as immigrants. From his humble beginnings as a farmer's son to an idealist college student at Tehran University to working odd jobs in the US, Varjavand takes the reader on an epic adventure and teaches us what it means to struggle and prevail. A must read for all who love this country.

John Naisbitt

Golden Apple Winner 2007

A lesson to learn from Reza's story is that no one needs to be a prisoner of his environment. One must be prepared to seize moments of opportunity. His early life was hard but his brothers made it possible for him to go to school, giving him a couple of Rials for lunch, coupled with his parents permission to go to school, if doing so did not interfere with his duties and if school did not inculcate in him notions that were in conflict with their religious beliefs—"anti-religious science." As I see it, this is a story worth telling for a couple of reasons: (1) it will be uplifting for children in developing countries whose daily lives Reza keenly, vividly, candidly describes, and (2) it will bring awareness in developed countries to the plight for disadvantaged children around the world.

In a broader context, the author speaks to the travails of life in his alley (neighborhood), as a proxy or representative of many such alleys, and perhaps even blocks, and cities in Iran. Reza's account of his mother's (being otherwise formally illiterate) tutoring of Quran provides insights into the role religion plays in an environment with afterworld imaginings, expectations, and musings.

Reza's writing style, sense of humor, and keen understanding of his own past all come through in this book. We see clearly the contrast between life in Iran and life in America he wants to turn our attention to. The book is at once entertaining and serious reading. As he shows, there is no need for both these things to be mutually exclusive. At every level, readers will be engaged with the conversation Reza has started and will benefit from the cultural socio-economic focus of the work.

Seymour Patterson, Ph. D.
Emeritus professor and author

Many Iranian writers in English suppress their inner Iranian, affecting Western attitudes for the benefit of the reader. Varjavand is the first to remain uncompromisingly Iranian, and in this way displays a refreshingly honest style of writing. His autobiographical work describes growing up in a poor neighborhood in the religious city of Qom and ending up an economics professor in the US. Yet his raw sincerity demotes the classical elements of rags to riches stories in favor of a modern style that showcases our ever globalizing culture. What is most exciting about Varjavand's writing is that he does not shy away from or apologize for using English to speak Persian. This writer is not into creating literary tourist attractions; you'll be lost sometimes, even insulted, but you'll come home bragging about having seen the real thing, tasted the real flavor and laughed the real laugh.

Ari Silets
Writer, Author

LaVergne, TN USA
17 November 2009

164392LV00003B/212/P